How to Train Your
German
Shepherd

liz palika

GERMAN
SHEPHERD

Photos by the author unless
otherwise credited.

The publisher wishes to thank the following owners and handlers of
the dogs in this book: Ralph Brown, Dan Gentile, Christine Lupton,
Dick Palazzo, David Scrivanic, and Anthony and Patricia Travers.

© Copyright by T.F.H. Publications, Inc.

Distributed in the UNITED STATES to the Pet Trade by T.F.H. Publications,
Inc., One T.F.H. Plaza, Neptune City, NJ 07753; on the Internet at
www.tfh.com; in CANADA Rolf C. Hagen Inc., 3225 Sartelon St. Laurent-
Montreal Quebec H4R 1E8; Pet Trade by H & L Pet Supplies Inc., 27 Kingston
Crescent, Kitchener, Ontario N2B 2T6; in ENGLAND by T.F.H. Publications,
PO Box 15, Waterlooville PO7 6BQ; in AUSTRALIA AND THE SOUTH PACIFIC
by T.F.H. (Australia), Pty. Ltd., Box 149, Brookvale 2100 N.S.W., Australia; in
NEW ZEALAND by Brooklands Aquarium Ltd. 5 McGiven Drive, New Ply-
mouth, RD1 New Zealand; in SOUTH AFRICA, Rolf C. Hagen S.A. (PTY.) LTD.
P.O. Box 201199, Durban North 4016, South Africa; in Japan by T.F.H.
Publications, Japan—Jiro Tsuda, 10-12-3 Ohjidai, Sakura, Chiba 285, Japan.
Published by T.F.H. Publications, Inc.
MANUFACTURED IN THE UNITED STATES OF AMERICA
BY T.F.H. PUBLICATIONS, INC.

contents

Introduction **4**

1 Selecting the Right Dog for You **6**

2 Canine Development Stages **18**

3 All About Formal Training **26**

4 Early Puppy Training **33**

5 The Basic Obedience Commands **44**

6 Advanced Training and Dog Sports **58**

7 Problem Prevention and Solving **74**

8 Have Some Fun With Your Training! **88**

Suggested Reading **94**

INTRODUCTION

I have been teaching dog obedience classes for over 20 years and see, on the average, more than a thousand dogs and owners per year. Through the years, I have seen a number of different breeds rise and fall in popularity. For a few years, German Shepherd Dogs were the rage; Poodles came and went, then Cocker Spaniels and Labrador Retrievers. Even though German Shepherds are no longer ranked number one on the American Kennel Club's popularity chart, they remain a very popular breed.

As an obedience instructor, I always have misgivings when people buy the "popular" breed, and German Shepherds are no exception. Now, don't get me wrong, most Shepherds are nice dogs! They were my first breed and my first love. My first obedience dog, first carting dog, first Frisbee™ dog, and first search and rescue dog was a German Shepherd. However, German Shepherds are not the

Traits that originally made German Shepherd Dogs trustworthy herders and guard dogs have made them one of today's most popular breeds.

german shepherd

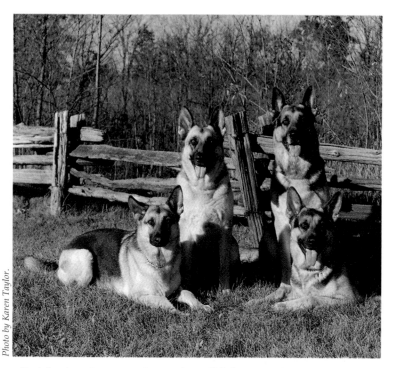

Training is an important element that will help ensure that your German Shepherd is a welcome and well-behaved addition to your family.

right dogs for everyone. Prospective dog owners need to understand the breed they are considering—whether it is a Lab, a Golden, a Cocker, or any other breed.

Prospective owners also need to know that there are other options than simply buying a puppy. Puppies are a lot of work and take a long time to grow up. Adopting an older puppy, a young adult, or even a mature dog might be a better choice for many people.

In this book, I have tried to present German Shepherd owners (and prospective Shepherd owners) with choices about choosing a dog and good effective information as to how to make that dog a well-behaved member of the family. Shepherds can be fun-loving, energetic clowns as well as serious, hard-working dogs. With training and help from their owner, they can be a friend, a partner, a protector, and a great companion.

german shepherd

SELECTING
the Right Dog for You

WHAT ARE GERMAN SHEPHERDS?

German Shepherds originated in Germany and were designed to be an all-purpose military and law enforcement dog as well as a herding dog. Hard-working, versatile dogs able to work in the roughest and most chaotic of conditions, the breed became a favorite of people needing a dog that could do anything.

The television, movie, and book heroes Rin Tin Tin and Strongheart helped make the breed more popular, and for a period of time, German Shepherd Dogs were ranked as one of the most popular breeds by the American Kennel Club. Unfortunately, that popularity has also caused problems. A German Shepherd is not the perfect dog for all people and all situations. They are beautiful, flashy dogs with a wonderful

German Shepherds are intelligent dogs with wonderful personalities, but new owners should take time to select the right dog for them.

Photo by Karen Taylor.

personality, and they have become popular as service dogs, therapy dogs, as well as obedience, agility, and flyball competition dogs. However, they are intelligent, thinking dogs that want to be close to people. Left alone in a backyard, the Shepherd will pace, cry, howl, bark, tear up the yard, dig tremendous holes, and try to escape. German Shepherds left alone for too long have also been known to mutilate themselves and develop immune system problems from depression. The German Shepherd is best for people who can spend time with the dog, give the dog a job of some kind, and who are dedicated to giving the dog the training it needs.

"The Shepherd is defined by his vitality and nobility; he is direct and fearless, confident and outgoing. The breed is poised and alert, well-fitting his many roles as man's helper and best friend," said Lowell Ackerman, DVM, of the breed (*Dr. Ackerman's Book of German Shepherds*, TFH Publishing, Neptune City, NJ 1996).

Temperament

German Shepherds are intelligent, energetic dogs. Very people oriented, Shepherds need to spend time with people

Many popular breeds require a good deal of time, attention, and care and German Shepherds are no exception.

to play, exercise, learn obedience skills and social rules, and even just have quiet time. This desire to be with people affects all aspects of his life. As was mentioned earlier, a Shepherd is not a good dog to be left alone in the backyard all day.

Bred to be protective, Shepherds make good watchdogs. Shepherds watch everything: the mail carrier, the meter reader, the neighborhood kids, and even the birds in the trees. Most will bark when people approach the yard or house, and although this is usually a desirable trait, German Shepherds must be taught how much barking is allowed and when to stop.

A well-trained, socialized German Shepherd can be an incredible working dog, sometimes serious to a fault. German Shepherds are the breed of choice for many guide

Exceptional working abilities and obedience skills have traditionally made German Shepherds ideal law enforcement and military dogs.

and service dog schools. Shepherds today are serving quite capably as guide dogs, service and assistance dogs, therapy dogs, law enforcement and military dogs, drug detection dogs, bomb detection dogs, arson detection dogs, and much, much more.

Don't let this ability to work fool you, though. Shepherds can find fun in anything. Puppies will play with anything—chasing butterflies, balls, toys, and even airplanes high in the sky. Even grown-up, mature adults retain a sense of fun and will turn into a clown when given any excuse to do so.

Physical Appearance

German Shepherds are medium-sized dogs, usually between 22 and 26 inches tall. The bitches (females) are smaller, lighter in weight and more feminine in appearance than the dogs (males). German Shepherds are incredibly strong for their size, with tremendous stamina. Shepherds have a thick double coat of medium length with the outer hairs straight and harsh, laying close to the body.

The most recognizable color seems to be the tan dog with a black saddle and black muzzle. However, the tan can range from a tannish-khaki color to a deep, rich chestnut, a silver-gray, or red; all with a black saddle or cape. All-black German Shepherds are also acceptable. All-white German Shepherds are very popular, too, with some people, but are

Although they are usually known for their black and tan markings, German Shepherds also come with all-black and all-white coats.

The German Shepherd is a strong, athletic dog, whose well-balanced body is built for working and activity.

not acceptable for conformation shows.

Besides color, one of the most recognizable features of a German Shepherd is his body shape. Whereas most dogs stand upright and square, German Shepherds have a longer back that slants down towards the tail. The back legs are quite angulated and when posed for conformation shows, one leg is stretched back farther than the other, which is set under the body. This body shape and leg angulation was to promote an athletic dog that could work all day and move in an easy, ground-covering trot. Unfortunately, breeding for this severe body conformation has caused the breed some problems. Many dogs have been produced with a variety of structural and skeletal disorders.

A German Shepherd should not just give the appearance of a well-balanced dog able to work hard, he should really be able to work. A healthy, sound German Shepherd should be able to jump a fence, leap for a Frisbee™, swim across a stream, and trot alongside your bicycle.

IS A SHEPHERD THE RIGHT DOG FOR YOU?

Evaluating Your Personality and Lifestyle

The decision to add a dog to your family is not a decision that should be taken lightly. This is a 14- to 15-year commitment, and German Shepherds are intelligent, intense dogs with some specific needs.

Do you work long hours, come home tired and just want to relax, spending the evening reading or watching television? If you do, then a calm, older Shepherd might be good for you. Do you come home tired but like to get outside, walking or riding your bicycle? If so, an adult dog might suit your needs. Do you work at home, have short work hours, and enjoy doing things? If so, a puppy or an active young dog should please you.

Being the center of a dog's world can be thrilling to some people and overwhelming to others. If you don't like being followed, watched, or touched, don't get a German Shepherd. A

Photo by Isabelle Francais.

German Shepherds need lots of daily exercise, whether it be swimming or running with you as you jog or ride your bike.

Shepherd will want to follow you from room to room and will be heartbroken even if you go to the bathroom without him. When you sit down, the Shepherd will want to lie on your feet. When you leave the house, the Shepherd will want to go with you. Obviously, having a dog with you 24 hours a day is impossible for most people; however, if you own a Shepherd you will need to be able to provide as much companionship as possible.

What is your life like? Are you retired and live alone? If so, and your health is good, either a puppy or an adult Shepherd might be good dog for you. Are there active children in the house? Shepherds can be wonderful with children as long as there is adult supervision and the dog is taught good social rules. However, if you work full time and live alone, a Shepherd

Consider your lifestyle before deciding to get a German Shepherd. Do you have the time and energy to train a puppy? If not, perhaps an adult dog would be better for you.

Photo by Isabelle Francais.

might not be the best choice—as was mentioned earlier, a Shepherd alone is a lonely, unhappy dog.

The Dog's Needs

Before you decide to add a German Shepherd to your family, make sure you can fulfill the dog's needs. First of all, your time and companionship is of the utmost importance. As was mentioned earlier, Shepherds do very poorly alone in a backyard all day. This is a companion breed that needs to spend time with you.

You will also have to have a securely fenced yard. As a protective working dog, Shepherds may try to get out of the yard to protect the front yard, or if alone, may try to escape to find you. A large, securely fenced yard is wonderful, but even a dog run (no smaller than 10 feet by 30 feet) is acceptable as long as the dog gets plenty of time out of the run with you.

You must also have some means of exercising the dog. If you like to go jogging, that's fine, but if you are not a jogger you will need to think of an alternative. Perhaps you can teach the dog to run next to your bicycle, or you can take the dog swimming on a regular

basis. A young, healthy Shepherd is *not* a couch potato!

MONEY MATTERS

Do you have the financial means to care for this dog? Good quality food is not inexpensive, nor is veterinary care. Your dog will need vaccinations, regular checkups and will need to be spayed or neutered. You will need grooming supplies, including brushes, nail clippers, and flea and tick control products. Your dog will need a collar, a leash or two, and a kennel crate. You will also need to invest in an obedience class (or two!). Also, at some point during the dog's lifetime, there may be an emergency veterinary call because of an injury or illness. You will need the financial resources to care for your dog and must never delay needed care because of a lack of money.

SELECTING THE RIGHT DOG

Male or Female?

There are a lot of myths concerning the personality traits of both males and females. Ultimately, it depends upon the personality of the individual dog.

Puppies are often too adorable to resist, but before you bring one home, be certain that you are ready for puppy teething, housebreaking, and training.

Spayed and neutered bitches and dogs are usually a little calmer than those that are not; spaying and neutering removes the sexual hormones and as a result, the sexual tension that can accompany those hormones. To be a good pet and companion, your Shepherd doesn't need those hormones anyway.

What Age?

Puppies are adorable, especially Shepherd puppies. When you add a puppy to your family it is just like adding a baby to your family. In fact, in many ways, raising a puppy is much like raising a child, except that the puppy will grow up faster. As the puppy learns and grows, it will become an intregal part of your family, and by the time your puppy has grown up (three years or so), your young German Shepherd will have become a good friend.

However, it takes a lot of work to raise a puppy and for many people, adding a puppy to their life might not be the best choice. But that doesn't mean those people cannot have a dog. There are many adult German Shepherds needing homes and these dogs could be just the answer for people who do not have the time to spend with a young puppy. With an adult dog, you know what you're getting. You know how big the dog is, what the adult personality is like, and the state of the dog's health. With a puppy, some of these things are unknowns until the puppy grows up.

There are, of course, some negative factors about adopting an adult dog. Adopting an adult is sometimes like buying a used car; you don't know how it has been treated prior to your ownership and that can affect future behavior. Many times, too, the adult dog's past health history is unknown. Newly adopted adult dogs also must have time to settle into their new homes; time must be allowed for emotional and physical adjustment.

Finding an Adult Dog

If you have decided that an adult Shepherd would be better for you, there are many places to find the right dog. Many Shepherds are given up by their owners for a variety of reasons; some didn't research the breed and found after a few months that a Shepherd was not the right breed for them. Other people may not have been willing to give their Shepherd the time and training the dog needed. Or

perhaps there was an emergency, the owner may have passed away and family members were unable to keep the dog. Check for these dogs at your local humane society or shelter.

RESCUE GROUPS

Many breed clubs also sponsor or run breed rescue groups. Rescue groups screen the dogs they take in for adoption. Dogs are checked for personality or temperament flaws (such as aggression) and their obedience skills (or lack thereof) are evaluated. The dogs are vaccinated, or, if needed, spayed or neutered. This screening process can be invaluable to you, the potential adopter. To find a Shepherd rescue group in your area, call your local humane society or shelter.

Once in a while, guide dog and service dog schools will have dogs available for adoption. There might be a young dog that washed out of the training program or an older retired dog that can no longer work. These dogs are normally very well socialized and incredibly well trained.

Evaluating an Adult Dog

Once you have found an adult German Shepherd that you like, how do you decide

Photo by Isabelle Francais.

Don't let your emotions take over when deciding on a dog or puppy, caring for a dog is a lifelong commitment.

whether this is the right dog for you? Well, emotions certainly play a part—do you like this dog? There is more of a chance of success in this new relationship if you and the dog like each other. However, there should be more to the decision-making process than just emotions.

Do you know why the dog was given up by his first owners? Sometimes the dog is given up through no fault of his own—maybe his owner was transferred overseas or his owner passed away. However, if the owner gave the dog up because of behavior problems, you need to know that. Has the dog had any obedience training? Is the dog housetrained? These are important issues because even if you are willing to do some training with the dog, housetraining a previously untrained adult Shepherd can be a tremendous task!

What is the dog's personality like? When you whistle or speak to the dog, does he look at you happily, wagging his tail? If he does, great. If he looks sideways at you, slinks, or bares his throat, be careful. He could be afraid or worried because of previous mistreatment, but an unknown fearful dog might also bite. Be careful, too, if the dog stares at you, making eye contact, without wagging his tail. This could be a potentially aggressive dog.

Ideally, you want a dog that is happy to see you without showing too much worry or fear and without showing any aggression. You want a dog that is housetrained and who has had some obedience training. Make sure that the dog's behavior problems are ones that you can live with for the time being and are willing to work on in the future.

Ideally, too, the dog has already been spayed or neutered, is vaccinated, and is healthy.

FINDING A PUPPY

If you have the time, resources, and patience to raise a puppy, you will want to find a reputable breeder. Breeder referrals can come from many sources. People walking their dog might refer you to their breeder. A veterinarian, groomer, or trainer may know of some reputable breeders. Many of the national dog magazines have classified ads where breeders can advertise. You might also want to attend a dog show in your community and talk to the people attending the show.

Once you find a few breeders, ask for an appointment to meet with them. At your meeting, ask the breeders a few questions. "Are you active in the dog world?" This answer will tell you many things. First, if the breeders show their dogs in conformation competition, their dogs are probably good examples of the breed. If they show in obedience competition, their dogs are trainable. If they show their dogs in herding trials, their dogs have the working instincts Shepherds were originally supposed to have. However, if they show their dogs in Schutzhund (protection) competition, their

dogs might be a little too reactive to make good pets.

"Do you belong to the German Shepherd Club of America as well as local or regional clubs?" If breeders do, they are more likely to be up to date on news about the breed. Breed club newsletters and magazines usually publish health-related issues, including many of the genetic or inherited problems that German Shepherds are prone to, as well as potential treatments.

Good, reputable breeders will stay up to date on health-related issues, which helps them to produce the best quality puppies.

"What health problems have you seen in your dogs?" If the breeders say none, be skeptical. A breed or line with no health problems is rare. German Shepherds can have a number of health problems, including hip and elbow dysplasia, joint

Photo graph by Isabelle Francais.

You can tell a lot about a breeder's puppies by watching their behavior. A submissive puppy may hesitate to play, but an energetic puppy may follow and come when he is called.

and bone disorders, epilepsy, allergies, and neurological disorders. Reputable breeders should be honest with you about potential health problems and what they are doing to try and prevent future problems.

"Can you provide me with a list of references?" Keep in mind that this list will consist of people the breeder knows are happy with their dogs, but it can still serve a purpose. You can still ask them about their experience. "Did the breeder work well with them? Would they buy from the breeder again?"

Caring breeders will ask you as many questions as you ask them. They want to know if you are the right person to buy one of their puppies. Don't get defensive; they are trying to do the right thing. Instead, answer the questions honestly. If by some chance, a particular breeder says that her dogs are not right for you, listen to her, she knows her dogs better than you do.

Evaluating a Puppy

Each puppy has his own personality and finding the right personality to match with yours is sometimes a challenge. For example, if you are outgoing, extroverted, and active, a quiet, withdrawn, submissive puppy would not fit well into your household and lifestyle. You will need a puppy more like you. On the other hand, that quiet puppy might do very well for a quiet person or a less active retiree.

When you go to look at a puppy or a litter of puppies, there are a few things you can do with the puppy to help evaluate his personality. First, with the puppy away from his mother and littermates, place the puppy on the ground and walk a few steps away. Squat down and call the puppy to you. An outgoing, extroverted Shepherd puppy will come happily and try to climb into your lap. If you stand up and walk away, the extrovert will follow you, trying to get underfoot. If you crumple up a piece of paper and throw it six feet away, he will dash after it and bring it back proudly. This Shepherd would do well with an owner who is just as much an extrovert as he is. He will need training, lots of exercise, and a job to occupy his mind.

A quiet submissive puppy will come to you when you call but may do a belly crawl, or may roll over and bare his belly. When you get up to walk away, the submissive puppy may watch you but may be hesitant to follow you. If you toss the piece of paper for him, he may go after it, bring it part way back, but may be hesitant to bring it directly to you. This

puppy will need a quiet owner, gentle handling, and positive training to build his confidence.

These two puppies are the extremes; most Shepherds are somewhere in between these personality types. Try to find a puppy with a personality that will be comfortable with you, your personality, your family, and your lifestyle. Don't get a pushy, dominant puppy and hope to change him; he may learn control with training but he will always have that personality. Nor should you get the quiet submissive puppy because you feel sorry for him. Find the puppy that is right for you.

BE CAREFUL!
Adding a dog to your family should be a time of anticipation and excitement, but it also requires thought, research, and preparation to prevent the experience from becoming a nightmare. Unfortunately, horror stories abound of purebred dogs plagued with health problems, or breeders who misrepresented their dogs or who didn't come through with the promised paperwork. Hopefully, this German Shepherd will be a part of your life for the next 12 to 14 years, so make sure a Shepherd is the right dog for you and choose it carefully.

Canine
DEVELOPMENT
2 Stages

IN THE BEGINNING

Even though dogs and people have lived together for thousands of years, the bond that we have with dogs must be renewed with each puppy. The bond itself is not hereditary although the tendency and ability to bond are. This relationship between a dog and owner is what makes owning a dog so special but it doesn't happen automatically. To understand when and how the bond develops, it's important to understand that a dog is a unique creature, not a person in a fuzzy dog suit.

FAMILIES AND PACKS

Most researchers agree that thousands of years ago the first domesticated dogs were descended from wolves. Wolves are very social creatures and live in an extended family pack. The pack might consist of a dominant male and a dominant female (usually the only ones who breed) as well as a few subordinate adults, juveniles, and puppies. This is a very harmonious group that hunts together, plays together, defends their territory against intruders and cares for each other and the pack's young. The only discord happens when there is a change in the pack order. If an adult of some status dies or leaves the pack, or if a youngster tries to assume dominance, there might be some jockeying around to fill that position.

Many experts feel that domestic dogs adapt so well to our lifestyle because we also live in groups, although our groups are called families instead of packs. However, the comparison really isn't accurate; our families are much more chaotic than the average wolf pack! We are terribly inconsistent with our social rules and rules for behavior. (We let the dog up on the couch when he's clean but yell at him when he jumps up with muddy paws!) To the dog our communication skills are confusing. Our voices say one thing while our body language says another. We tell "white lies" to spare someone's feelings; our dogs don't

German Shepherds are such loving and social creatures that it won't take long for you to develop a strong and lasting bond with your dog.

understand "white lies." To our dogs, people are very complex, confusing creatures. So, yes, we can say that both dogs and humans live in social groups and we can use that comparison to understand a little more about our dogs; however, we must also understand that our families are very different from a wolf pack.

FROM BIRTH TO FOUR WEEKS OF AGE

For the first three weeks of life, the family and the pack are unimportant as far as the baby German Shepherd is concerned. The only one of any significance is his mother. She is the key to

his survival and is the source of food, warmth and security.

At four weeks of age, the baby Shepherd's needs are still centered on his mother but his littermates are becoming more important. Littermates provide warmth and security when mom leaves the nest. During this period he will learn to use his senses to follow sounds and to focus his eyes. His curiosity about the world around him is developing and he will start exploring his nest or whelping box.

Mom will also start disciplining the puppies now and her instinctive training is vitally important to the puppies' future acceptance of discipline and training. We can also learn a lot by watching Mom discipline her babies.

MOTHER LOVE

Ebony is a black and dark red German Shepherd, an American Kennel Club Champion and an obedience Utility Dog. She is also a very good mother. When one of her puppies bites too hard, her correction is short, sharp, fair and firm: a growl and a muzzle bite that ceases as soon as the puppy reacts submissively. Every correction is followed by love and affection and she never holds a grudge.

The breeder should also be handling the puppies during this period, gently touching and massaging them. The puppies will learn the difference between their Mom's caresses and those from people.

WEEKS FIVE THROUGH SEVEN

The baby Shepherd goes through some tremendous changes between five and seven weeks of age. He is learning to recognize people and is starting to respond to individual voices. He is playing more with his littermates and the wrestling and scuffling teach each puppy how to get along, how to play, when the play is too rough, when to be submissive, and what to take seriously. Mom's discipline at this point teaches the puppy to accept correction, training and affection.

This is a good time for the puppy to meet other people. The breeder should supervise all visits so that the puppy isn't handled too roughly or frightened. Of course, friendly handling and play will help socialize the puppy to people.

If the puppy is taken from his mother and littermates during this time frame, he may have lasting behavioral problems. He may have difficulty dealing with other dogs, may have problems accepting rules and discipline and may turn excessively shy or aggressive because of fear.

THE EIGHTH WEEK

The eighth week of life is a frightening time for most puppies. Puppies go through several fear periods during their growing up and this is the first one. Even though this is the traditional time for most puppies to go to their new homes, they would actually benefit tremendously by staying with their mom and littermates for one more week. If the puppy leaves his breeder's home during the eighth week of life and is frightened by the car ride to his new home, he may retain that fear of car rides for the rest of his life. The same applies to his new home, new sounds in the house, the trip to the veterinarian's office or anything else that frightens him.

It's important for your German Shepherd puppy to socialize with other littermates in order to learn how to interact with other dogs.

Photo by Isabelle Francais.

WEEKS NINE TO TWELVE

The baby Shepherd can go to his new home anytime during the ninth and tenth weeks of life. At this age, he is ready to form permanent relationships. Take advantage of this and spend time with your new puppy, playing with him, cuddling with him, and encouraging him to explore his new world. Teach him his name by calling him in a happy, high-pitched tone of voice, especially when he is already moving toward you. (Never use his name to scold him!) Encourage the puppy to follow you by backing away from him, patting your leg or clapping your hands.

Socialization is very important now. Socialization is more than simply introducing your puppy to other people, dogs, noises and sounds. It is making sure that your baby Shepherd is not frightened by these things and that he is introduced to them gradually. For example, after your baby Shepherd has had some vaccinations (check with your veterinarian), take your puppy with you to the pet store when you go to buy some dog food. While there, introduce your puppy to the clerks, other customers, and even to the store parrot. Your trip there could also include walking up some stairs, walking on slippery floors and going through an automatic door. All of these things, introduced gradually and with a lot of encouragement, and repeated all over town, add up to a confident, well-socialized puppy.

RETRIEVING

Begin retrieving games at 9 to 12 weeks of age. Throw a toy about six feet away and encourage him to chase it. When he grabs the toy, call him back. Praise him enthusiastically when he gives it to you. If he runs away and tries to turn it into a keep-away game, stop playing. Don't chase him! Let him learn that he must play by your rules. Chasing a ball or soft flying disc can be good exercise for your puppy and it sets the stage for a sound working relationship later.

During this time frame, pack instincts are developing and you can use this stage of growth to teach your puppy his position in the family. Each and every day, have each member of the family roll the puppy over and give him a tummy rub. This exercise may seem very simple but by baring his tummy, he is assuming a submissive

To ensure that your puppy is confident and well socialized, be sure to introduce him to new people, places, and experiences.

position to family members. When his mom corrected him, he would roll over and bare his tummy to her; here, he's doing it for you.

When your baby Shepherd is 11 or 12 weeks old, discipline becomes more important. Love, attention and security are still vital, of course, but your puppy is now ready to learn some basic household rules. Don't allow him to do anything now— such as stealing food, jumping on people, or bouncing off the furniture— that you are not going to want him to do when he's fully grown.

WEEKS THIRTEEN THROUGH SIXTEEN

From 13 through 16 weeks of age, your puppy will be trying to establish his position in your family pack. Consistency in enforcing the household rules is very important and everyone in the family should be doing

things the same way. If he senses a soft heart or a weak link in the chain of command, he will take advantage of it. Dominant-personality puppies may start mounting behavior to small children or toys. This should be discouraged consistently; don't let it happen! Socialization to other people, dogs, and experiences should be continued. Make sure the experiences are positive.

WEEKS SIXTEEN THROUGH TWENTY SIX

Sometime between 16 and 20 weeks of age, many dogs go through another fear period,

In the process of trying to establish his position within the family pack, your Shepherd puppy may break some rules. Don't let him forget that you are the boss!

much like the one they had at eight weeks of age. Things the dog accepted as normal previously might become scary. A friend's German Shepherd walked out into their front yard and started barking at a potted plant that had been there, in the same spot, since he was a baby. It was like he just suddenly noticed it and decided it was frightening!

During this fear stage, don't reinforce his fear. If you cuddle him and tell him, "It's okay, sweetie," he will assume that you are praising him for his fearful reaction. In other words, you are praising the fear; the fear response was right! Instead, walk up to whatever is scaring him and touch it as you tell him, "Look at this." Walk him up to it if you can without frightening him too much. Help him overcome his fear instead of reinforcing it.

Many young Shepherds discover their protective instincts at this time, too. If your puppy Shepherd starts showing signs of protectiveness (growling, snarling, raised hackles) interrupt his behavior by distracting him or turning him away. If you encourage this behavior, or correct it too harshly, you will put too much emphasis on it and your puppy

may continue to do it. Too much emphasis may result in overprotectiveness or fearfulness in your dog as he grows up. Instead, react with calmness and just stop it from happening.

If you want your Shepherd to be protective later, as many people do, don't worry. This training will not hamper those instincts. However, at this age, your puppy really doesn't know what to protect against and what not. So instead of letting him take over, stop his behavior and show him that you are in charge, not him. Later, when he's more mature, you can encourage the specific protectiveness you want.

Photo by Isabelle Francais.

Protective instincts emerge early in German Shepherds, but that type of behavior should be discouraged until your dog is more mature.

THE TEENAGE MONTHS

The teenage months in dogs are very much like the teenage years in children. Adolescents in their teens are feeling strong, striving to prove their ability to take care of themselves and trying to become independent. At the same time, they want the security of home. Those two conflicting needs seem to drive some teens (and their parents) absolutely crazy! Dogs can be very much the same way, pushing the boundaries of their rules, testing you to see if you will enforce those rules. Many Shepherd owners say that during this stage of growing up, their Shepherd simply acts "entirely too full of himself!"

The teenage stage in German Shepherds hits at any time between eight and ten months of age, lasting until 12 to 14 months old, and you will know when it happens! One day you may ask your previously trained young dog to sit and he will act as if he has never heard the word before in his life! Your previously well-socialized dog may start barking or growling at other dogs, or may start pushing your children around. You may have previously taught your Shepherd to stay off the furniture, but during this stage he may climb up there anyway and ignore you, or in extreme cases, may even growl at you when you scold him.

You will need to consistently enforce your household rules during this stage. Hopefully, you have already started obedience training and if you have, make sure you practice those skills regularly. If you have not yet started training, do so now, it's not too late.

Make sure your dog regards you as his leader. You can reinforce that idea by some things you do around the house. For example, you should always go through doors first. The dominant dog, alpha wolf, or leader of the pack always goes first. You should eat first, too. You should go up the stairs ahead of your dog; don't let him dash up the stairs and turn around and stare at you. If he does, he is assuming the dominant position!

Something else you can do is to give him permission to do things, even if he was going to do them anyway. For example, if he picks up his ball and is bringing it to you to throw, tell him, "Good boy to bring me your ball!" If he lies down at your feet, tell him, "Good boy to lie down!" By giving him permission and praising him, you are telling your dog that you have control.

It is very important you understand that your dog's adolescent behavior is natural— it is a part of growing up—and is not directed at you personally. You must also remember that this too shall pass. Your Shepherd will grow up—someday!

GROWING UP

German Shepherds are generally not considered fully mature—mentally and physically—until they are three years old. Sometimes the bitches (females) will mature a little earlier, at maybe two-and-a-half years, but usually the dogs (males) take a little longer. After the teenage stage, before maturity, your Shepherd may go through some different behavioral stages. There may be

Patience and proper training throughout your puppy's early stages will be worth the results—a well-trained and lovable German Shepherd.

another fear period—usually at about a year-and-a-half of age. Handle this one just like you did the others; don't cater to your dog's fear, just work him through it.

There may be another period of challenging—seeing if you really are the boss—at about two years of age. Treat this as you did the teenage stage; enforce the rules and praise what he does right.

Sometimes there is a time when your Shepherd may act somewhat territorial, protective, or even aggressive. Handle this just like you did when he was younger and did the same thing. Turn him away, distract him, or have him do something else, but don't overreact. If you do overreact and correct him too hard, he may get the wrong message—"Wow! Something is wrong!"—and that could cause his behavior to get worse.

When your German Shepherd reaches the age of three years, he (or she) is generally considered to be grown up. However, grown up to a Shepherd does not necessarily mean life is serious; he may be serious when he needs to be (or wants to be) but life to a German Shepherd is still great fun! So enjoy!

All About
FORMAL
Training

WHY IS TRAINING IMPORTANT?

Why did you decide to add a German Shepherd to your family? You probably wanted a companion, a friend, a protector, and a confidant. You may have wanted a dog that could do things with you: run along the beach, catch tennis balls, and hike in the mountains. To do any of these things your Shepherd will need training.

Many dog owners won't admit their dog needs training. "He does everything I ask," they say. Yet when asked specific questions about their dog's behavior, the answer changes. A trained dog won't jump on people, dash out the door each time it is opened, or raid the trash can.

Dog owners can benefit from training, too. Dog owners learn how to teach their dogs, how to praise them, and how to encourage good behavior. They also learn how to prevent problem behavior from happening and how to correct the mistakes that do occur.

Dog training is much more than the traditional sit, down, stay, and come. Dog training means teaching your Shepherd that he is living in your house,

Not only are training classes a great way to teach basic obedience, they are also the perfect place for your Shepherd to interact with other dogs.

not his. It means that you can establish some household rules and expect him to follow them. It will not turn your Shepherd into a little (or big!) furry robot; but it will cause your dog to look at you in a new light. Training will cause you to look at him a little differently, too. Dog training is not something you do to your Shepherd; instead it is something the two of you do together.

TRAINING METHODS

Talk to a dozen dog trainers (someone who trains dogs) or dog obedience instructors (someone who teaches the dog owner how to train his or her dog) and ask them how they train and you will get a dozen different methods. Any trainer or instructor who has been in business for a period of time is going to work out a method that works for her. Each method will be based upon the trainer's personality, teaching techniques, experience, and philosophy regarding dogs and dog training. Any given method may work wonderfully for one trainer but may fail terribly for another.

Because there are so many different techniques, styles, and methods, choosing a particular instructor can sometimes be

difficult. It is important that you understand some of the different methods so that you can make a reasonable decision.

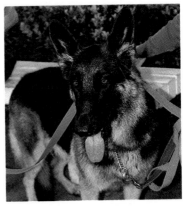

When looking for a training class, talk to instructors about their experience and training methods. Take care to choose the class that is right for both you and your dog.

Compulsive Training

Compulsive training is regarded as a method of training that forces the dog to behave. This is usually a correction-based type of training; sometimes with quite forceful corrections. This training is often used for law enforcement and military dogs and can be quite effective for hard-driving, strong-willed dogs. In most cases, it is not the best training method for softer dogs. Many pet dog owners do not like this style of training and often feel that it is too rough.

Inducive Training

This training is exactly the opposite of compulsive training; instead of being forced to behave, the dog is induced or motivated toward proper behavior. Depending upon the instructor, there are few or no corrections used. This training technique works well for many puppies, for softer dogs and sometimes for owners who dislike corrections of any kind. Unfortunately, this is not the technique for all dogs (especially all Shepherds) because some Shepherds will take advantage of the lack of corrections or discipline.

MIDDLE OF THE ROAD

The majority of trainers and instructors use a training method that is somewhere in the middle of these two techniques. An inducive technique is used when possible, while corrections are used as needed. Obviously, the range can be vast, with some trainers leaning toward more corrections and others using as few corrections as possible.

GROUP CLASSES OR PRIVATE LESSONS?

There are benefits and drawbacks to both group classes and private lessons. In group classes, the dog learns to behave around other distractions, specifically, the other dogs and people in the class. Since the world is made up of lots of things capable of distracting your dog, this can work very well for most dogs and people. In addition, group classes work much like group therapy for the dog owners. The owners can share triumphs and mishaps, and can encourage and support one another.

The drawback to group classes is that for some dogs the distractions of the group are too much. Some dogs simply cannot concentrate, especially in the beginning. For these dogs, a few private lessons may help enough so that he can join a group class later. Dogs with severe behavior problems—especially aggression toward other dogs or people—should also bypass group classes for obvious reasons.

Private lessons work well for dogs with specific problems such as aggressive behavior. Private training is also good for dogs who are too distracted in a group setting or for dog owners who are reluctant to speak up in a group class. The downfall of private training is the lack of distraction, and for many instructors the goal of

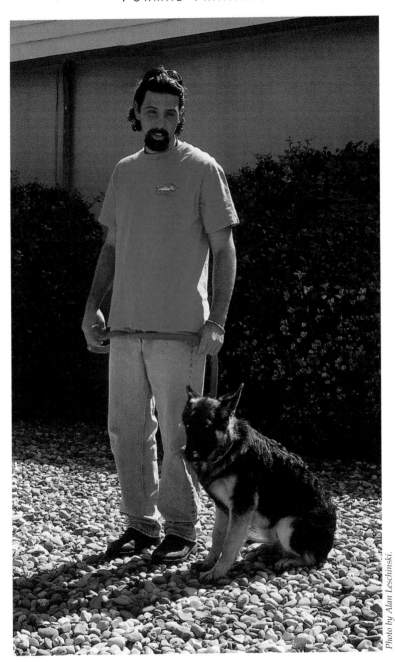

Photo by Alan Leschinski.

From sit to down to stay, the training program you choose should equip you with the commands necessary to achieve your personal training goals.

german shepherd

private training is to get the dog and owner to the point that they can eventually join a group class.

Photo by Alan Leschinski.

Puppy classes cover housetraining and basic commands as well as provide an environment for your young Shepherd to socialize with other puppies and people.

WHAT ARE YOUR GOALS?

There are an unlimited number of things you can train your Shepherd to do. It's up to you to decide what you would like to do and then find a training program to help you achieve those goals. Do you want to teach your dog to be a well-behaved house dog and companion? Do you want to compete in obedience trials? Would you like to do field trial work? Perhaps you would like to share your dog with others and participate in a therapy dog program. Think about your goals and then keep them in mind as you and your dog start training.

Puppy Class

Puppy or kindergarten classes are usually for puppies over 10 weeks of age but not over 16 weeks. These classes are half training and half socialization. The puppy's owner learns how to housetrain his puppy, how to set up some household rules, and how to prevent problems from happening. The puppy learns some basic commands like sit and come. In addition, the puppy gets a chance to socialize and play with the people and puppies attending the class.

Basic Obedience Class

This class is usually for dogs over four months of age. In this class, the dogs and their owners work on the basic obedience commands, including sit, down, stay, heel, and come. Most instructors also spend time discussing problem prevention and problem solving, especially the common problems like jumping on people, barking, digging, and chewing.

Dog Sports Training

Some instructors will offer classes preparing your dog to participate or compete in dog sports. These are the classes to take if you and your Shepherd will be competing in obedience, agility, flyball, or other dog sports.

HOW TO FIND AN INSTRUCTOR OR TRAINER

When trying to find a trainer or instructor, word-of-mouth referrals are the best place to start. Although instructors can place an advertisement in the yellow pages or newspaper, a fancy ad is no guarantee of expertise. However, happy customers will demonstrate their experience with well-behaved dogs and will be glad to tell you where they received their instruction.

Have you admired a neighbor's well-behaved dog? Ask where they went for training. Call your veterinarian, local pet store, or groomer and ask who they recommend. Make notes about each referral. What did people like about this instructor and what did they dislike?

Once you have a list of referrals, start calling the instructors and ask a few questions. How long has she been teaching dog obedience classes? You will want someone with experience, of course, so

that she is capable of handling different situations that may arise. However, experience alone is not the only qualification. Some people that have been teaching for years are still teaching exactly the same way and have never learned anything new.

Ask the instructor about German Shepherds; what does she think of the breed? Ideally, she should be knowledgeable about Shepherds, what makes them tick, and how to train them. If she doesn't like the breed, go elsewhere.

ADVANCED TRAINING

Advanced training classes vary in content depending upon the instructor. Some offer classes designed to teach your dog to work off leash, while others emphasize hand signals or other commands. Ask the instructor what she offers.

Ask the instructor to describe her training methods. Does this sound like something you could be comfortable with? Ask if there are any alternative techniques used. Not every dog will respond to training the same way; every instructor should have alternative methods.

Does the instructor belong to any professional

organizations? The National Association of Dog Obedience Instructors (NADOI) and the Association of Pet Dog Trainers (APDT) are two of the more prominent groups. Both of these publish regular newsletters to share information, techniques, new developments, and more. Instructors belonging to professional organizations are more likely to be up-to-date on training techniques, styles, and so forth, as well as information about specific dog breeds.

Make sure, too, that the instructor will be able to help you achieve your goals. If you want to compete in obedience, make sure she can either help you towards that end goal, or can refer you to someone else who can.

After talking to the instructors, ask if you can watch one of their classes. If the instructor says no, then cross her off your list. There should be no reason why you cannot watch one class to see if you will be comfortable with this style of training. As you watch the class, watch how she handles the students' dogs. Would you let her handle your dog? How does she relate to the students? Are people relaxed? Are they paying attention to her? Do the students seem to be making progress?

After talking to the instructors and watching a class, you should be able to make a decision as to what class you wish to attend. If you are still undecided, call the instructors back and ask a few more questions. After all, you are hiring her to provide a service, and you must be comfortable with your decision.

Don't forget that training should be a positive experience for you and your dog. Use this time to build a stronger relationship with your German Shepherd.

BONDING

Training helps build a relationship between you and your dog. This relationship is built on trust, affection, and mutual respect. Training can help your dog become your best friend; a well-mannered companion who is a joy to spend time with and one who won't send your blood pressure sky-high!

Early
PUPPY
Training

BLANK SLATE

A puppy is like a blank slate, or in this era's terms, a blank, newly formatted computer disk. What you teach the puppy in his early months will have bearing on the rest of the puppy's life. Therefore, it's important to keep in your mind a vision of what your dog will grow up to be. Although Shepherds are medium-sized and are not giant breeds, many do get quite large. They are still strong, powerful dogs and you need to keep this in mind. At ten weeks of age, your Shepherd puppy would love to cuddle on your lap, but will you really want him to do that when he's 75 pounds of muscle, hard elbows, and rough paws? By establishing some basic rules early, your puppy will grow up understanding them, which will prevent potential problems from developing later.

CRATE TRAINING

By about five weeks of age, most puppies are starting to toddle away from their mom and littermates to relieve themselves. You can use this instinct to keep their bed clean, and with the help of a crate you can housetrain your Shepherd puppy.

A crate is a plastic or wire travel cage that you can use as your Shepherd puppy's bed. Many new Shepherd owners shudder at the thought of putting their puppy in a cage, "I could never do that!" they say. "It would be like putting my children in jail!" A puppy is not a child, however, and he has different needs and instincts. Puppies like to curl up in small,

Although your puppy may look cute and harmless now, it's important to begin training early before problem behavior develops.

Photo by Isabelle Francais.

close places. That's why they like to sleep under the coffee table or under a chair.

Because your Shepherd puppy does have an instinct to keep his bed clean, being confined in the crate will help him develop more bowel and bladder control. When he is confined for gradually extended periods of time, he will hold his wastes to avoid soiling his bed. It is your responsibility to make sure he is never left too long.

The crate will also be your Shepherd puppy's place of refuge. If he's tired, hurt, or sick,

Crate training is the easiest and fastest way to housetrain your German Shepherd puppy.

allow him to go back to his crate to sleep or hide. If he's overstimulated or excited, put him back in his crate to calm down. Because the crate does physically confine the puppy, it can prevent some unwanted behaviors, such as chewing on electrical cords or slippers.

INTRODUCING THE CRATE

Introduce your puppy to the crate by propping open the door and tossing a treat inside. As you do this, tell your puppy, "Go to bed!" and let him go in to get the treat. Let him investigate the crate and go in and out freely. When your puppy will go in after the treat and has sniffed the crate thoroughly, offer a meal in the crate with the door propped open. The next meal can be offered in the crate and this time close the door behind him, but let him out as soon as he has finished eating. Offer several meals in the same fashion; this is to show your puppy that the crate is a pretty neat place.

After your puppy is calmly eating in the crate, start feeding his meals back in the normal location and go back to offering him a treat or toy for going into the crate. Continue teaching him the phrase, "Go to bed."

Don't let your puppy out of the crate for a temper tantrum. If he starts crying, screaming, throwing himself at the door, or scratching at the door, correct him verbally, "No! Quiet!" or simply close the door to the room and walk away. If you let him out for a temper tantrum,

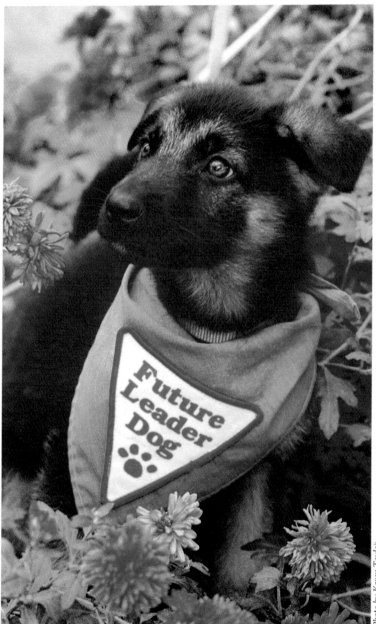

German Shepherds often serve as herding, law enforcement, and therapy dogs; early puppy training is the first step to ensuring that your young Shepherd follows in the breed's tradition.

german shepherd

you will just teach him that temper tantrums work. Instead, let him out when you are ready to let him out and when he is quiet.

Crate Location

The ideal place for the crate is in your bedroom within arm's reach of the bed. This will give him eight uninterrupted hours with you while you do nothing but sleep. In these busy times, that is quality time! Having you nearby will also give your puppy a feeling of security. If you exile him to the backyard or garage, he will be more apt to cry, whine, howl, pace, or get into trouble because of loneliness and fear. Instead, keep him close.

Having your puppy close at night will also save you some wear and tear. If he needs to go outside, you will hear him and can let him out before he has an accident. If he's restless or bored, you can rap the top of his crate and tell him to be quiet.

HOUSETRAINING

One of the most common methods of training a puppy is paper training. The puppy is taught to relieve himself on newspaper and then, at some point, is retrained to go outside. Paper training teaches the puppy to relieve himself in the

To prevent housetraining disasters, don't let your inquisitive puppy have the run of the house. Crates and dog runs are ideal for teaching him the rules.

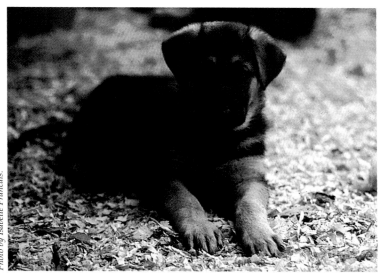

Photo by Isabelle Francais.

german shepherd

Your puppy's daily routine should include a schedule of eating, eliminating, walking, sleeping, and playing.

Photo by Isabelle Francais.

house. Is that really what you want your Shepherd to know?

Teach your puppy what you want him to know. Take him outside to the area where you want him to relieve himself and tell him, "Go potty!" (Use any command comfortable for you.) When he has done what it is he needed to do, praise him, "Good boy to go potty!" Don't just send your Shepherd puppy out into the back yard and hope that he does what he needs to do; you may let him back into the house just to see him squat on the rug! You need to go with him to see that he has relieved himself, that he does so in the correct area, and so you can praise him for doing so!

Successful housetraining is based upon setting your puppy up for success rather than failure. Keep accidents to a minimum and praise him when he does relieve himself where he should go.

Establish a Routine

Your Shepherd puppy is a creature of habit and routines are important. Housetraining is much easier if there is a set routine for eating, eliminating, playing, walking, and sleeping. A workable schedule might look like this:

• **6:00 am**—Dad wakes up and takes the puppy outside.

After the puppy relieves himself and dad praises him, Dad fixes the puppy's breakfast, offers him water, and then takes him back outside.

- **7:00 am**—Mom goes outside to play with the puppy before getting ready for work. Just before she leaves, she brings the puppy inside, puts him in his crate, and gives him a treat.

- **11:00 am**—A dog-loving neighbor who is retired comes over, lets the puppy out of his crate and takes him outside. The neighbor knows the puppy's training, so he praises him when he relieves himself. He throws the ball for the puppy, pets and cuddles him, and then gives him a treat when he puts him back in his crate.

- **3:00 pm**—Daughter comes home from school, lets the puppy out into the backyard while she changes clothes. After calling her friends on the phone, she goes out back with the puppy, throws the ball, cleans up the yard a little, and then takes the puppy for a walk. When they get back, she brings the puppy to her bedroom while she works on her homework.

- **6:00 pm**—Mom takes the puppy outside to go potty, praises him, and then feeds him dinner.

- **8:00 pm**—After daughter plays with the puppy she takes him back outside.

- **11:00 pm**—Dad takes the puppy out for one more chance to go potty before going to bed.

The schedule you establish will have to work with your normal routine and lifestyle. Just keep in mind that the puppy should not remain in his crate longer than three to four hours, except at night. The puppy will need to relieve himself after eating and drinking, after exercise and playtime, and when waking up from a nap.

PUNISHMENT

If you try to housetrain your puppy by punishing him for accidents that happen in the house, either by rubbing his nose in his mess (a commonly used correction) or by sharply scolding him, you run the risk of confusing him more than teaching him. If you correct your puppy for housetraining accidents, he may feel that going potty is wrong, and he may start being sneaky about where he goes so that you can't catch him. You may start finding "surprises" in strange locations around the house or yard. Keep in mind that the act of relieving himself is not what is wrong—he has to do that— it is relieving himself in the house that is the problem.

Limit the Puppy's Freedom

Many puppies do not want to take the time to go outside to go potty, especially if there are interesting things happening in the house. Those puppies will then sneak off somewhere—a back bedroom or behind the sofa—to relieve themselves. By limiting the puppy's freedom you can prevent these "accidents" from happening. Close bedroom doors and use baby gates across hallways to keep your puppy close. If you can't keep an eye on him, put him outside or in his crate.

By establishing household rules as soon as your new German Shepherd joins your family, your puppy is more likely to develop into a well-behaved dog.

Household Rules

It's important to start establishing some household rules as soon as your new puppy joins your household. Your puppy, at eight to ten weeks of age, is not too young to learn, and by starting early you can prevent problems from getting started. When deciding what rules you want to establish, look at your puppy, not as the baby he is now, but the adult he will grow up to be. You may not mind if your Shepherd puppy is on the couch now, but are you going to want him up there when he's full grown? Do you want him jumping on people? A full grown Shepherd is powerful enough to knock over kids, senior citizens, and even adults not paying attention.

Some common household rules might include teaching your puppy not to jump on people, to behave when guests

PRACTICE PATIENCE

New puppy owners seem to invite advice. Everyone has a method of housetraining that works better or faster and is more reliable than anyone else's method. Ignore your well-meaning friends. Shepherd puppies need time to grow up and develop bowel and bladder control. Establish a routine that works well for you and stick with it. If you stick with the schedule, your puppy will progress. However, don't let apparent success go to your head; don't assume he is housetrained. Too much freedom too soon will result in problems.

come over, to stay out of the kitchen, and not to chew on inappropriate things. In addition, you might want to teach the puppy to leave the kids' toys alone, to ignore dirty clothes, and to stay off the furniture.

To teach your puppy what is allowed and what is not, you must be very clear with your commands and corrections. Either something is right or it is wrong. When the puppy picks up his toy instead of your slippers, praise him, "Good boy to play with your toy!" When he picks up your slipper, correct him, "No! That's not yours!" Take the slipper away and then give him one of his toys, "Here this is your toy!" Let him know what is wrong, then follow it by showing him what he can do instead and praise him when he does it.

ACCEPTING THE LEASH

All dogs need to accept the restraints of a leash, and this can be hard for some puppies. If your Shepherd puppy is frightened by the leash, he may resent the leash for the rest of his life. Therefore you want to introduce the leash calmly and positively.

Soon after you bring your puppy home, put a soft nylon

Photo by Alan Leschinski.

Start gradually, with short sessions, and your German Shepherd should grow accustomed to the feel of his leash.

or cotton buckle collar on him. Make sure it's loose enough to slip over his head should he get tangled up with something (as Shepherd puppies are known to do!) After a day or two, when he is no longer scratching at the collar, attach a leash to the collar and let him drag it around the house for 10 or 15 minutes, while you watch him to make sure it doesn't tangle on something. While the puppy is dragging the leash, he will step on the leash, feel the tug on his neck and just generally get used to the feel of it.

After two or three sessions of dragging the leash, you can teach your puppy to follow you when you have the leash in hand. Have a few pieces of a soft treat you know he likes, such as hot dog or cheese. Let him sniff the treat while you back away and verbally encourage him, "Let's go! Good boy!" When he follows you for a few feet, stop, praise him, and let him have a bite of the treat. Shepherds are the original, proverbial food hounds and training with treats for these dogs makes training much easier!

Repeat the exercise two or three times and quit for this session. Reward your puppy by throwing the tennis ball a few times. After two or three training sessions like this, start making it more challenging by backing away from your puppy faster or by adding turns or zigzags. If he balks or acts confused, stop and go back to the simple routine again until he understands.

INTRODUCING THE CAR

Many puppies are frightened by riding in the car because the car took them away from mom and their littermates and the car takes them to the veterinarian's office where scary things happen. You don't want this idea to blossom, though; you want your puppy

to understand that riding in the car can be a good thing.

Start by lifting your puppy into the car and handing him a good treat. As soon as he has eaten the treat, lift him down and walk away. Repeat that sporadically over several days. Then lift him into the car, give him a treat and let him eat it, then let him explore the car a little. After he has sniffed a little, give him another treat, let him eat it, and lift him out of the car. Continue this type of training for a week or more, depending upon how nervous your puppy is about the car.

No matter how carefully you housetrain your puppy or older dog, accidents will happen. Be prepared with a non-toxic, effective stain and odor remover.
Photo courtesy of Francodex.

When your puppy is expecting a treat in the car, put his crate in the car and strap it down so that it won't bounce around or go flying in an emergency situation. Put your puppy in his crate, give him a treat, and close the crate door and the car door. Start the engine, back the car out of the driveway and then drive back up to the house. Give your puppy a treat and let him out of the crate. The next time, drive down the street and back, then around the block. Increase the time and distance of the drives very gradually.

PRAISE
Never stop the training session when your Shepherd puppy is confused. Instead, always stop the training session on a high note. Do something you know he can do and do well, then stop, praise him enthusiastically, and play ball with him for a few minutes.

Keep in mind that you want your puppy to anticipate good things in the car, not scary things. Your dog will have a lifetime of car rides ahead of him, and life will be much nicer if he can enjoy the rides.

Once your puppy has learned to enjoy social handling, you can—after his bath and during his massage—groom him with brushes or a hair dryer.
Photo courtesy of Metropolitan Vacuum Cleaner Co., Inc.

Tummy rubs and massages can also be used to calm an excited or overstimulated puppy. He'll love the attention!

SOCIAL HANDLING

Your puppy cannot care for himself; you must be able to brush him, pull burrs and foxtails out of his coat, clean his ears, and trim his nails. Unfortunately, your Shepherd puppy doesn't understand that cleaning his ears is necessary and he may struggle and fight when you try to do these things. The social handling exercise will help teach your puppy to accept your care.

Sit on the floor and have your puppy lay down between your legs. He can lay on his back or his side and get comfortable. Start by giving him a slow, easy tummy rub; the idea here is to relax him. If he starts to wiggle or struggle, gently restrain him with one hand as you massage him with the other.

When the puppy is no longer struggling, start giving him a massage. Start at his neck and ears and gently massage the muscles. Work down his neck to his shoulders, down each front leg to the paw. Touch the paw gently but firmly (some dogs are ticklish) and touch each toenail. Go back to his body and massage the back, the ribcage, and the hips. Work down the back legs just like you did his front legs. And then give his tail a little massage as well.

Once your puppy has learned to enjoy this handling, you can—during the massage—check his ears and clean them when needed, brush him, check for fleas or ticks, trim his toenails, comb out burrs, or even medicate him when necessary.

CALMING DOWN
Social handling can even be used to calm an excited or over-stimulated puppy. If you let your puppy in from the backyard and he is just bouncing off the walls with excitement and energy, you have a couple of choices. If you try to correct the puppy, he will probably just get more excited. However, if you grab him and lay him down, then start massaging him, he will relax. In addition, you are giving him the attention he wants and needs from you.

The Basic
OBEDIENCE
Commands

TEACHING YOUR GERMAN SHEPHERD

Teaching your Shepherd is a process. Unfortunately, you cannot simply tell your dog to sit and expect him to do it. First of all, until he has been taught what the word "sit" means, it is simply an unknown sound. To confuse training even more, he has no idea why you want him to sit, nor does he know why it is so important to you. Therefore, teaching becomes a process.

You want to show your dog what it is you want him to do. Help shape him into the sit if that is what you are teaching, or move him off the furniture if that is your focus. Then, as you are helping him, teach him the word, "Sit," or "Off the furniture." Praise him when he does it right, even if you have helped him, "Good boy to sit!" or "Good boy to get off the furniture!"

Praise him every time he does something right. Your dog will work harder and do more for you when you use a lot of praise. That doesn't mean that you should give undeserved

praise; Shepherds are very intelligent and your dog will figure it out. Instead, give enthusiastic praise when he makes an effort and does something right for you.

DON'T PRACTICE INCORRECT BEHAVIOR

Interrupt incorrect behavior or action when your dog is thinking about it or starts to move. If you have asked him to sit and he does, but then starts to sniff and lean as if he is going to get up, interrupt him, "Don't do it!" When he looks at you, tell him, "That's good to sit!"

Do not correct your dog until you are sure he understands what you are asking him to do. After he understands and is willing to obey the command, you can correct him with a verbal correction or a quick snap and release of the leash when he chooses not to do it. Use only as much correction as needed to get his attention and no more. With corrections, less is better! German Shepherds resent too harsh or undeserved force and will show that with their behavior, sometimes to the point of fighting back.

Interruptions and corrections alone will not teach your dog; they are used only to stop—at that moment—undesirable behavior or actions. Your dog learns much more when you reward his good behavior. So stop what you don't want, but lavishly praise what you do want!

Timing is vitally important as you teach your dog. Make sure you praise him as he is doing something right and interrupt or correct him as he is making a mistake.

The sit command is the basis for the other commands you will use in training. You may need to shape your Shepherd into a proper sit position.

SIT AND RELEASE

The sit is the foundation command for everything else you will teach your Shepherd. When your Shepherd learns to sit and sit still, he is also learning to control himself. Learning self-control is a very hard lesson for many young Shepherds; being still is simply not in their genetic code! However, your Shepherd can learn to control himself and the sit command is the place to start.

The sit is also the foundation command for many other exercises, including the down and wait, as well as many advanced obedience commands. The sit is also great around the house. Your Shepherd cannot jump up on people if he is sitting. He cannot knock his food bowl out of your hand at dinnertime if he's sitting. You can fasten his leash to his collar more easily if he is sitting still. It's a useful command!

There are two methods to teach your Shepherd to sit. Some dogs work better with one method than they do with the other, so try both and see which will be better. Hold your Shepherd's leash in your left hand and have some treats in your right hand. Tell your Shepherd to sit as you move your right hand (and the treats) from his nose over his head towards his tail. He will lift his head to follow your hand and will sit in response to that movement. As he sits, praise him, "Good boy to sit!" Pet him while he's in the sitting position, give him a treat and have him hold the sit until you pat him on the shoulder to release him, "Release!" We want this release command to tell your dog that he is finished with that particular exercise and can move. You will be using the release with several different exercises.

If your dog is too excited by treats to concentrate on sitting, or if he spins around in place to get the treat instead of sitting, then try the second technique. Tell your Shepherd to sit as you put your right hand on the front of his chest as your left hand slides down his back to his rump and you gently shape him into a sit. Praise him for sitting, pet him quietly, and do not allow him to pop back up. If he does, shape him back into position. If he is very wiggly, keep your hands on him as you praise him for sitting, then, with your hands on him, you can gently restrain him so that he cannot pop back up. When you are ready for him to move from the sit, pat him on the shoulder and tell him, "Release!" Don't

get into the habit of repeating your commands. If you tell your dog to sit three or four times, which one should he listen to? You are not teaching him sit by repeating it, but you are teaching him that he doesn't have to listen to you. Is that really what you want him to learn? Instead, give each command only once and then help your dog to succeed. Tell him to sit, wait a heartbeat to allow him to do it, and help him do it if he doesn't.

BE FAIR

Make sure you are very clear as to what you want from your dog. Remember, something is either right or wrong to your dog; it's not partially right or partially wrong. Be fair with your demands, your praise, and your corrections.

DOWN

The down exercise continues one of the lessons the sit exercise started, that of self-control. It is hard for many young, bouncy Shepherds to control their own actions but it's a lesson that all must learn. Practicing the down exercise teaches your Shepherd to lie down and be still.

Start with your Shepherd in a sit. Rest one hand gently on his shoulders and have a treat in the other hand. Let him smell the treat and then tell him, "Dog, down" as you take the treat straight down to the ground in front of his front paws. As he follows the treat to the ground, use your hand on his shoulders to encourage him to lie down. Praise him, give him the treat, have him hold the position for a few moments, and then release in the same manner that you did from the sit. Pat him on the shoulder and tell him, "Release!"

If your Shepherd looks at the treat as you make the signal but doesn't follow the treat to the ground, simply scoop his front legs up and forward and lay him down. The rest of the exercise is the same.

As your Shepherd learns what the down command means, you can have him hold it for a few seconds longer before you release him but do not step away from him. Stay next to him and if you need to, keep a hand on his shoulder to encourage him to remain lying down.

STAY

When you taught your Shepherd to sit and to lie down, you taught him to move into those positions and to hold still until you released him. The stay

The steps of the down exercise are simple: Start in a sit, motion him down with a treat on the ground, then praise him and reward him with the treat.

command continues those exercises by teaching your dog to hold still for gradually increasing times as you move away from him. Eventually your Shepherd will be able to hold the sit or down stay for several minutes (longer in the down) and when you are a distance away, maybe even in another room.

Start by having your Shepherd sit. With the leash in your left hand, use the leash to put a slight bit of pressure backwards (towards his tail) as you tell him, "Dog, stay." At the same time, use your right hand to give your dog a signal that will mean stay—an open hand gesture with the palm towards your dog's face. Take one step away and at the same time, release the pressure on the leash. If your Shepherd moves towards you, gets up, or lies down, tell him "No," (so that he understands he has made a mistake) and put him back into position. Repeat the exercise. After a few seconds—and a few seconds only—step back to your dog and praise him. Don't let him move from position until you give him the release command.

You can use the same process to teach your dog to stay in the down position. Have

him sit, then lie down. Give him the hand signal and the verbal command to stay while putting slight pressure backwards on the leash. Take one step away as you release pressure on the leash. If he moves, tell him "No," and put him back into position. After a few seconds, go back to him, praise him, and then release him.

With the stay commands, you always want to go back to your dog to release him. Don't release him from a distance or call him to come from the stay. If you do either of these, your dog will be much less reliable on the stay; he will continue to get up from the stay or will start to anticipate the release

Once your dog is in the sit position, you can use a signal, an open hand with the palm toward your dog's face, to indicate the stay command.

Photo by Alan Leschinski.

The stay command teaches your dog to remain still until you release him; it can be used in either the sit or the down position.

from a distance. When teaching the stay, you want your dog to understand that stay means "Hold this position until I go back to you and release you." No confusion and no questions asked.

As your dog learns the stay command, you can increase the time he holds the stay. However, make sure you increase the time very gradually. If your dog is making a lot of mistakes, moving often, you are either asking your dog to hold the stay too long or your dog doesn't understand the command yet. In either case, go back and reteach the command from the beginning, very gradually increasing the time that you ask him to hold the stay.

Increase the distance you move away from your dog just as gradually. Again, if your dog is making a lot of mistakes, make sure he understands what you are asking him to do. Then, increase the distance one step away at a time.

SOCIAL GRACES OF THE STAY COMMAND

When your Shepherd has learned the basics on the stay, start using the down stay around the house. Have your dog down stay while you are eating so that he isn't begging under the table or stealing food from the kids. Have him do a down stay when guests come over so he isn't jumping all over your guests. There are a lot of practical uses for this command; just look at your normal routine and see where they can work for you.

Once your Shepherd understands the stay command and you know that he understands it, you can start correcting mistakes. As has been mentioned before (and will be mentioned again!) young Shepherds are wiggly, bouncy creatures that have a hard time holding still. Self-control is a skill that must be learned. If your Shepherd is having a hard time holding still, keep the stay short in time and distance.

Correct excess movement with a sharp verbal correction and a snap and release of the leash. When your dog does hold the stay, especially when he has been having a hard time, praise him enthusiastically!

WATCH ME

The watch me exercise is a very useful command that teaches your Shepherd to ignore distractions and focus on you. This will be particularly useful when you and your dog are out in public and he gets excited by children playing, dogs barking, or birds flying overhead.

Start by having your dog sit in front of you. With the leash in your left hand, have a treat in your right hand. Let your dog smell the treat and then take it up to your chin as you tell him, "Dog, watch me!" When his eyes follow your hand to your face and he looks at you, praise him, "Good boy to watch me!" Give him the treat and release him from the sit. This is a particularly hard exercise for many young Shepherds, so try teaching it first in the house,

Eye contact is an important element in training. The watch me exercise teaches your German Shepherd to focus on training commands and ignore distractions.

Photo by Karen Taylor.

where there are fewer distractions. Make sure your dog can do it and understands it well before moving on to the next step.

Once he will watch you while you practice in the house, move outside where there are more distractions. If he knows the command and ignores you, take his chin in your left hand as you give the signal with your right. Help him to look at you. If he still struggles against you, use a verbal correction. When he looks back at you, praise him.

When your dog will watch you outside with a few distractions you can move on to the next training step. Start with your dog sitting in front of you, give him the command "Watch me" and then start walking backwards. Encourage him to follow you and watch you at the same time. After six steps (or so) stop and have him sit, then praise him enthusiastically! After a few tries, back up a little farther, then add turns and zigzags. Make it challenging and when he can watch you, make the praise worthwhile—tell him what a wonderful dog he is!

Photo by Alan Leschinski.

The heel exercise teaches your dog to walk beside you without pulling. Once he masters the heel, your Shepherd will be able to maneuver turns and changes in pace.

HEEL

When your Shepherd can watch you while you walk backwards, then you are ready to teach the heel. Heel will mean, "Walk with me, by my left side, with your neck and shoulders by my left leg. You will pay attention to me and walk as I do: slow, fast, normal, left turns, right turns, and anything else." Obviously, this is a complicated exercise. However, if your Shepherd is watching, it won't be too hard.

To start, practice a watch me exercise as you have been doing it; backing away from your dog. When he is following you and paying attention, simply turn your body—as you are walking—so that you and your dog end up walking forward together with him on your left side. Picture this in your mind—you are backing away from your dog, your dog is facing you, following you. Back to your dog's right as you continue walking. You and your dog should end up facing the same direction with your dog on your left. This is the heel. When you stop, have your dog sit.

If your dog starts to pull forward while you are walking, simply back away from him and encourage him to follow you again. If you need to, use the leash to make sure he follows you quickly. Praise him when he

Problems with the heel command and leash training can be eliminated by using a halter especially designed for dogs that pull. It's like having power steering for your dog.
Photo courtesy of Four Paws.

The heel exercise will help prepare your Shepherd for more advanced exercises and training.

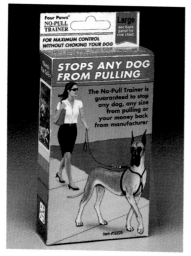

does. When his attention is back on you, turn into the heel position again. Don't be upset if you have to back away a few times. In fact, the more you do it, the better. Your dog will pay more attention to you if he's not quite sure where you will be going.

When your dog is walking with you nicely, then you can start eliminating the backing away. Start the heel with your dog sitting on your left side and tell him, "Watch me! Dog, heel!" and start walking. Praise him when he's walking nicely with you. If he starts to pull, you can correct him, "Dog, no pull!" However, if he is intent upon pulling or is distracted, simply back away from him and turn him away from whatever is distracting him.

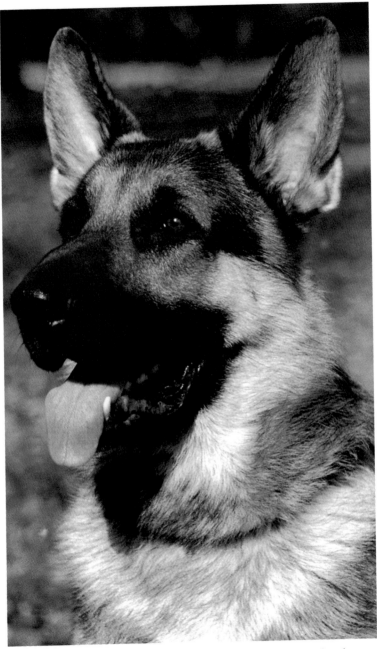

Once your German Shepherd is trained, you'll appreciate the results of your patience and hard work: a well-behaved and obedient companion.

COME

With a Treat

The come command is one of the most important commands your German Shepherd needs to know. Not only is the come important around the house and yard, but should he be out in front of your house, the come command could save him from dashing into the street and getting hit by a car. If you take him out to run, or you decide to do obedience work with him, he must have a good, reliable come.

Because the come command is so important, you will use two different techniques for teaching it. The first method will use food treats to teach your Shepherd that the come is fun and will result in a treat, which is something near and dear to all Shepherds! Take a small plastic container, like a margarine container, and put some dog food kibble in it so that it makes a nice plastic rattling sound. Then, have some treats in hand that you know your dog really likes—something special. Shake the container and ask your dog if he wants a treat, using the word he already knows for treat, such as cookie, biscuit, or bone. "Dog, do you want a cookie?" Then

Enticing your Shepherd with a small container of treats is one of two ways to teach him the come command. Once your dog understands the command, you can eliminate the treats.

pop a treat in his mouth and praise him, "Good boy! Yeah!" The praise and the treat teach your dog that the sound of the container means he should come to you for something good. Do this for several days until your dog comes running whenever he hears the container rattling.

At that point, you can shake the container and say, "Dog, Come! Cookie!" This builds a relationship between the words cookie and come. After a few days, drop the word cookie altogether and simply shake the container, say, "Dog, come!" and pop a treat in his mouth and praise him.

Practice this command two or three times per training session, several times a day. Don't do it too many times each session or it will lose its appeal. However, you do need to practice it a lot so that the dog reacts to it automatically, without even thinking about what he's doing.

Some people have reservations about this technique because they are worried that their dog will not come to them when they don't have a treat. First of all, you will be using two different techniques to teach your Shepherd to come. Later, when

Photo by Alan Leschinski.

Do not allow your German Shepherd off-leash freedom until he obeys you consistently and reliably.

your dog is coming reliably every time you call him, you will be able to get rid of the treats, although it is important to use them as long as you need them. In addition, this technique—when taught properly—can produce such a wonderful, strong reliable come that it is worth all your efforts.

With the Long Line

The second method will teach your dog to come when he's a little farther away from you. It will also help teach your Shepherd to come to you on those instances when you don't have the treat container. In

A reliable come is required for further obedience training; it may also prevent your German Shepherd from running after people or cars.

addition, it teaches your dog that he doesn't have a choice, he *has* to come to you when you call him.

With this technique, you will need a 20- to 30-foot length of cotton clothesline rope. Don't use nylon; it is too rough on your hands. Fasten the rope to your dog's collar and let him go play. When he is distracted by a bird or his toys, call him, "Dog, come!" If he comes to you right away, praise him enthusiastically. If he does not come directly to you, do *not* call him again. Simply pick up the rope, back away from him, and using the rope, make him come to you. The key to this is to verbally praise him even if you have to drag him in to you. The come has to be positive; if he thinks he's going to get into trouble by coming to you, he won't come at all. You have to praise him and let the long line be the bad guy.

After you have praised him, release him and let him go play again. In a few minutes repeat the exercise all over again. Practice this in the back yard and in the front yard, even in the house if he plays keep away in the house. Teach your dog that he must come to you the first time you call him, every time you call him.

Photo by Alan Leschinski.

If your dog does not come to you when called, you may have to use his leash to pull him toward you. Always reward your Shepherd no matter how he comes to you.

Don't allow your Shepherd freedom off leash in an unfenced area until he is well trained, grown up, and mentally mature enough to handle that responsibility. Many dog owners let their dogs off leash much too soon, and the dog learns that he can run away from them or play keep away, staying just out of reach. Each time he does this, he learns that he can, and there is nothing you can do to change his mind. Therefore, leave him on leash or on a long line until he is well trained and grown up. For some German Shepherds, that might be two-and-a-half or three years old.

USE IT OR LOSE IT!

The best way to make this obedience training work for you and your Shepherd is to use it. Training is not just for those training sessions; instead, training is for daily life. Incorporate training into your daily routine. Have your Shepherd sit for dinner and for treats. Have him lie down and stay during meals or when company comes over. Have him sit and stay at doorways so that he isn't dashing out open doors. Use these commands and make them a part of your life. They will work better that way.

Advanced
TRAINING
and Dog Sports

One of the great things about dog training is that you are never finished; there is always more you can teach your dog. Would you like your Shepherd to behave himself off leash? You can teach him that. Wouldn't teaching him to recognize and respond to some hand signals be fun? It is. Your dog can learn hand signals for down, sit, stand, stay, and more, including directions left and right.

Before you start teaching any of these commands, make sure he is proficient in the basic commands. He should be able to respond to the sit, down, stay, and heel (on leash) with one command and very few corrections. Ideally, he should also come to you when you call (off leash in the house or fenced yard) using the shaker and a verbal command. If your dog is still having some trouble with the basics, work on those some more before going on to other commands.

HAND SIGNALS

When you start teaching your Shepherd hand signals, use a treat in your hand to get his attention and use the verbal command he already knows to help him understand what you want. As he responds better and starts to show some understanding of the command, you can then make the verbal command softer, giving the hand signal first, and eventually stop saying a verbal command altogether.

The difficult part of teaching your dog hand signals is that in the beginning he may not understand that there is some significance in your motions. After all, people move their

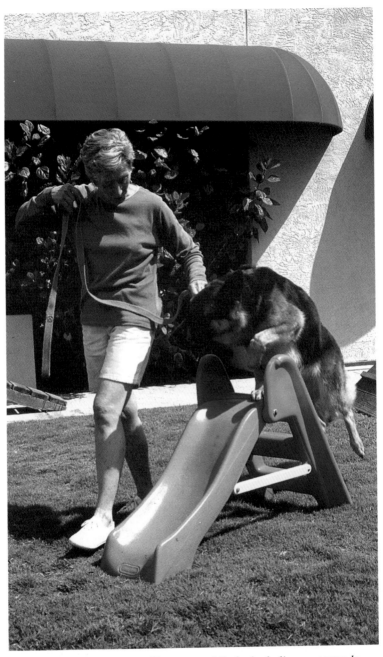

Once your German Shepherd has mastered the basic obedience commands, you can move onto advance training, sports, and other fun activities.

hands constantly, especially when they are talking, and your dog may not realize that those motions could mean something. Also, for hand signals to work, your dog must be watching you!

Down

When you taught your Shepherd to lie down by taking a treat to the ground in front of his feet, you were starting to teach him a hand signal. Granted, he was watching the treat in your hand, but he was also getting used to seeing your hand take the treat there. That motion of your hand is a signal, a command that can mean the same thing as your verbal

In advance training, a hand signal is often used without a verbal command. This Shepherd knows the signal for down.

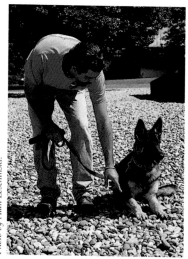

command, "Down." Continue using the treat in the beginning; don't get rid of the treat until you are sure that he knows the signal and is following the hand signal reliably.

Start teaching him by practicing the down command with the signal as you taught him earlier. Have him sit, tell him, "Down" and take the treat to the ground in front of him. When he's down, praise him and release him. If he's doing this well, with no hesitation, give him the signal and delay your whispered verbal command by a couple seconds. If he lies down for your signal, praise him enthusiastically! If he waits for your verbal command, try it again with more emphasis on the signal.

When he can follow the signal with no verbal command, start making it more challenging. Continue to have him sit, but stand in front of him and then signal him to lie down. Walk a leash length away and try it. Try it from across the room. Remember to praise him enthusiastically when he follows your signal and lies down.

Sit

If you were able to teach your Shepherd to sit using the treat above his nose, you were starting to teach him a signal that means sit. If you weren't able to use that technique, don't worry, he can still learn a sit signal.

With your Shepherd on the leash held in your left hand, have a treat in your right hand, and standing in front of him, take the treat from his nose up to your left shoulder so that your forearm is up and across your chest. At the same time, tell him, "Dog, sit" in a soft voice. If he hesitates, give him a jiggle of the leash and collar. If he refuses, tell him to sit again and snap and release the leash. When he sits, praise him, give him the treat, release him, and try it again.

Stay

When you taught your Shepherd the stay command earlier, you were again introducing him to a hand signal. When you said, "Dog, stay," and put your open palmed hand in front of his nose, that was a hand signal. In fact, this signal is so obvious your dog will probably obey it right away with little extra training. Try it by having your dog sit, then give him the stay signal without a verbal command and see what happens. Did he hold it? If he

did, go back to him and praise him. If he didn't, put him back where he started, give him the signal again, and quietly tell him to stay.

With hand signals, it is even more important to maintain consistent eye contact with your dog. Continue to practice the watch me command to reinforce your dog's attentiveness.

Photo by Alan Leschinski.

Come

The come signal will start with your right hand and arm straight out to your side at shoulder height. Bring it around to your chest as if you were reaching out to get your dog and bringing him to you. Finish it by making the sit signal; up and across your chest, so that when your Shepherd comes dashing to you, he will see the sit signal and sit in front of you.

Start teaching it by having the come shaker in your right hand, shaking it slightly as you make the arm signal and quietly tell your dog to come. You may also need to quietly tell your dog to sit as you finish with the sit command. He isn't used to watching more than one command at a time. When he comes and sits, praise him enthusiastically and give him a treat.

Watch your dog and when he seems to understand the signal, take away the shaker and practice the signal with a quiet verbal command. Continue to pop a treat in his mouth when he does come. Gradually eliminate the verbal command but continue to praise and reward him for coming to you.

Once your dog has mastered the come exercise with the verbal command and treats, try the exercise with just the hand signal.

german shepherd

Only after your Shepherd has consistently obeyed your commands should you give him off-leash freedom.

OFF-LEASH CONTROL

One of the biggest mistakes people make with their dogs is to take them off the leash too soon. When your dog is off leash, you have very little (or no) control and your dog will learn very quickly that he can get away from you and there's nothing you can do about it. Shepherds are very inquisitive dogs and love to explore. More than one Shepherd has been so involved in his exploring that he has forgotten he should have been paying attention to his owner.

Before he is allowed total off-leash freedom (outside of your house or fenced in yard) you need to make sure that his training is sound. That means he understands the basic commands and responds to them reliably.

Your German Shepherd must also be mentally mature enough to handle the responsibility of off-leash freedom. Mentally mature means that he is through the challenging adolescent stage of growing up. Most Shepherds are not mentally adults until they are two-and-a-half or three years old, some even older. Until then they are still very puppy-like and don't take much of anything seriously. There's nothing wrong with this; many people love puppies, even big puppies! However, puppies do not have the concentration, responsibility, and seriousness to be allowed off-leash freedom.

USING THE HAND SIGNALS

When your dog has a good understanding of the hand signals, you can start putting them together and using them in groups as part of your training sessions. Have your Shepherd come, sit, down, and then come again. Praise him enthusiastically and reward him with a treat. Or rearrange the order; have him lie down, then come back up to a sit, then come and lie down again. Challenge your training skills and his learning and attention skills.

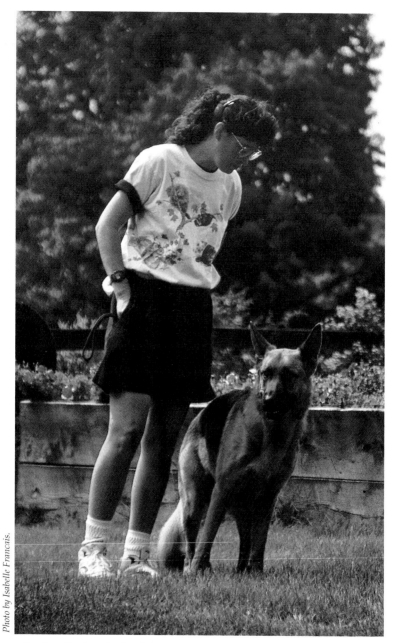

Photo by Isabelle Francais.

Don't make the mistake of allowing your German Shepherd freedom from his leash too soon; your dog must be well trained and mature enough to handle the responsibility.

german shepherd

64

Photo by Alan Leschinski.

With enough training and practice, your Shepherd should respond to the come signal without the use of a leash. Until then, however, you may have to pull him with the line.

The Long Leash and the Come

The long leash that was introduced earlier in the section on teaching the come command is a good training tool for teaching off-leash control. You used the long leash to teach your dog to come to you when he was at a distance (but within reach of the long leash) from you. Review that training session by putting your Shepherd on the long leash, and while holding one end of it let him go play. When he is distracted and not paying attention to you, call him to come and then back away from him so that he gets a chance to chase you. (The chase is exciting to most dogs and this will make the come more exciting.) If he doesn't

immediately start to come to you, use the long leash to give him a snap and release. If he is still ignoring you, reel him in like a fish on a fishing pole. When he gets to you, either under his own power or yours, you must praise him. The come must be rewarded; however, if he comes to you voluntarily, the praise should be much more enthusiastic!

Heel

In most public places, dogs are required to be on leash; however, the off-leash heel is a required part of obedience competition. It has some practical uses, too. If your Shepherd is well trained, you

Your dog must be able to perform the off-leash heel in order to participate in obedience competitions. Gradually eliminate his leash until he has mastered the exercise.

Photo by Alan Leschinski.

Photo by Alan Leschinski.

Once your German Shepherd is heeling reliably on his leash, you may try to do off-leash exercises.

can tell him to heel and walk him to your car or the mailbox without worrying about a leash. What happens if you are out on a walk and the leash breaks? Or his collar? It's happened before and will happen again. If your dog can heel by your side without a leash and collar, you won't need to panic.

Hook two leashes up to your dog's collar—his normal leash and a second, very lightweight leash. Do a watch me with treats, then practice his heel work, having him walk nicely with you as you walk slow, fast, normal, and turn corners. Stop and have him sit while you praise him. Then reach down and unhook his regular leash

and toss it to the ground in front of him. If he bounces up, thinking he's free, correct him, "I didn't release you!" and bring him back to the sit position. Hook his regular leash back up and repeat the exercise.

When he sits still for the leash to be tossed to the ground, continue by telling him to heel and then practice his heel work as you did with both leashes. Stop, have him sit, put the regular leash back on and repeat the whole thing again. Go back and forth between one leash and two so much that he won't remember what he has on. Repeat this over several training sessions. Remember to use the watch me command

Your Shepherd needs encouragement throughout his training, as well as a flexible and patient teacher.

Photo by Alan Leschinski.

DOG SPORTS

Have you discovered that you like training your German Shepherd? A lot of Shepherd owners start with puppy or basic training and discover that it is a lot more fun than they expected. For those who like training, there are a lot of dog sports that you and your Shepherd can participate in. Some are just for fun, some are recreational, others are competitive, and a couple are performed as services for people.

Conformation Competition

The American Kennel Club and the United Kennel Club all

In conformation competition, judges will compare your Shepherd to the standard of the breed.

Photo by Isabelle Francais.

with treats to help keep his attention on you.

When he is to the point of behaving himself, regardless of the leash or leashes, take off the second leash. Fold his regular leash up and tuck it under his collar over his shoulder blades, so that it is on his back. Practice his heel work. If he makes a mistake or tries to take advantage, grab the leash on his back.

Expect (and demand) the same quality of work off-leash that you expect when he's working on leash. Don't make excuses for mistakes off leash. Once your dog has mastered off-leash control, there is a whole new world waiting for you both: dog sports!

award conformation championships to purebred dogs. The requirements vary between the registries, but basically the championship is earned when a purebred dog competes against other dogs of its breed and wins. When competing, the judge compares each dog to the standard for that breed and chooses the dog that most closely represents the written description.

This is a very simplistic explanation, however. If you feel that your Shepherd might be a good conformation candidate, write to either the American Kennel Club or the United Kennel Club and ask for information about competing in conformation. You will also want to do some reading on your breed and compare your dog to the written standard. You may also wish to attend a few dog shows in your area and watch the conformation competition to see if this is a sport that you would be interested in.

Obedience Competition

Obedience competition is a team sport involving you and your dog. There are set exercises that must be performed a certain way, and both you and your dog are judged as to your ability to perform those exercises. Many, many German Shepherds have done very well in obedience.

Both the American Kennel Club and the United Kennel Club sponsor obedience competition. There are also independent obedience tournaments—not associated with either the AKC or the UKC—held all over the country.

Again, you may wish to attend a local dog show and watch the obedience competition first. If this is something you would like to do, write to the AKC or UKC for a copy of their obedience competition rules and regulations. You will also need to find a dog trainer in your area that is experienced in obedience competition training to help you. There are also many books on the market that can help you prepare for competition.

Canine Good Citizen

The Canine Good Citizen program was introduced by the American Kennel Club in an effort to promote and reward responsible pet ownership. During a Canine Good Citizen test, the dog and owner must complete a series of ten exercises, including sitting still for petting and grooming, walking nicely on a leash, sit, down, stay, and come. Upon completion of all ten exercises, the dog is awarded the title CGC.

For more information, contact the American Kennel Club or a dog trainer in your area.

Flyball

Is your Shepherd, like so many others, absolutely tennis ball crazy? If so, then flyball is the sport for you. In flyball, dogs compete on a team. The dogs race over a course of

AGILITY

Agility is a fast-growing and popular dog sport that combines a grand prix jumping event with an obstacle course. The dog must run through, jump over, and otherwise complete a series of obstacles in a set order. The dog is judged both by his manner of completing the course (safety is stressed) and how quickly he ran.

The American Kennel Club, the United Kennel Club, and the United States Dog Agility Association sponsor agility competitions; write to them for rules and competition information.

Agility competitions test your Shepherd's intelligence and coordination with a series of jumps and obstacles.

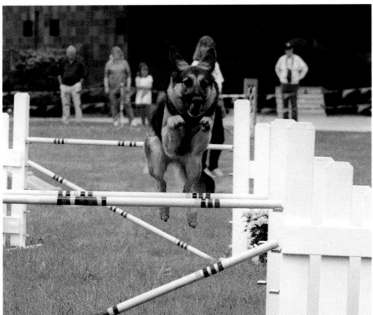

Photo by Karen Taylor.

hurdles, hit a machine that tosses a tennis ball, grab the ball, and race back over the hurdles. The team that finishes first wins. Flyball has become so popular in some parts of the country that tournaments are held on a regular basis with numerous teams competing.

If your Shepherd is tennis ball crazy, contact the North American Flyball Association for competition rules.

Temperament Test

The American Temperament Test Society was founded to provide breeders and trainers with a means of uniformly evaluating a dog's temperament. By using a standardized test

SCHUTZHUND

Schutzhund is a sport that originated in Germany for the purpose of testing the working abilities of German Shepherds and other German working dogs. It combines obedience, tracking, and protection work. Schutzhund trials are held all over the country.

with each dog being tested in exactly the same manner, the test can be used as a means of comparing and evaluating potential breeding stock, future working dogs, or simply as a way for dog owners to see how their dog might react in any given situation.

German Shepherds are intelligent, hard-working dogs that can be trained to perform any number of work tasks.

Photo by Isabelle Francais.

german shepherd

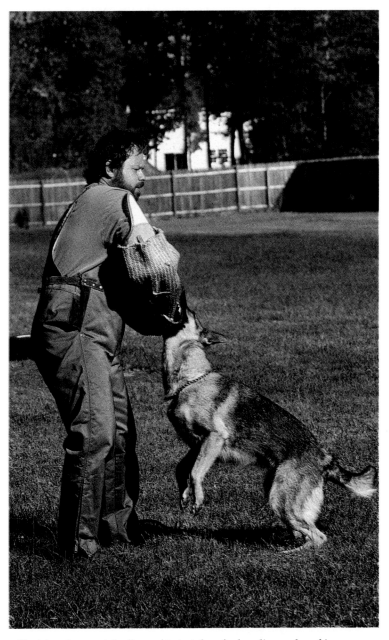

Shutzhund was originally used to test dogs for breeding and working abilities. Today, Shutzhund competitions evaluate tracking, obedience, and protection.

For more information about the test and a schedule of tests in your area, write to the American Temperament Test Society.

Therapy Dogs

Although dog owners have always known how important our dogs are to us, researchers have now reported that dogs are good medicine. Therapy dogs provide love, affection, warmth, a sense of touch, and motivation to people who need it. Therapy dogs visit hospitals, nursing homes, day care centers, and hospices.

Your dog provides great companionship and warmth to you, why not to others? Consider entering your Shepherd into a therapy dog program.

Children and puppies were clearly made for each other. However, if you're not certain how your Shepherd will react in a situation, you can have his temperament tested.

Scent Work

Does your Shepherd use his nose to discover the world? Most do. German Shepherds have wonderful scenting abilities and have been used in many working situations because of this talent. Shepherds have been trained to detect flammable substances and participate in arson investigations. Shepherds are used to find bombs, illegal drugs, and even illegal foods coming into the country from abroad or over the border. A US Customs Service Shepherd named Snag has intercepted

Photo by Isabelle Francais.

Photo by Judith Strom.

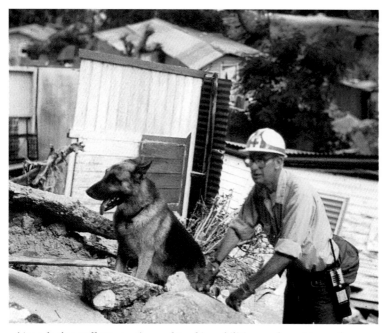

Your dog's excellent scenting and tracking abilities can be put to good use in search and rescue work.

millions of dollars in illegal drugs. You can use your dog's scenting abilities, too, in tracking and in search and rescue work.

Tracking competitions are offered by the American Kennel Club, with titles awarded for different levels of performance. Contact a dog trainer in your area for information about tracking classes or training. Write to the AKC for rules and regulations pertaining to tracking.

Search and rescue work in non-competitive, volunteer humanitarian work requires a great deal of training for both the dog and the owner, but it is extremely rewarding work. There is nothing more important than saving a life.

Because of their sensitive noses, German Shepherds have been trained to detect flammable substances, illegal drugs, and bombs. Scent discrimination will allow your German Shepherd to fine tune his abilities.

Problem
PREVENTION
and Solving

German Shepherds are very intelligent dogs that learn quickly and retain what they have learned very well. Because of these traits, some Shepherd owners are very surprised when their dog develops problem behaviors. "He knows that digging up the lawn is wrong so why does he do it?" one owner asked me. Another owner said, "My dog goes absolutely berserk in the evenings, running from one end of the house to the other, and he doesn't care if he knocks anything or anyone over as he dashes past. Why?" Unfortunately, those and other questions regarding problem behavior aren't always easy to answer.

Most of the behaviors that you might consider a problem—such as digging, barking, jumping on people, chewing, and so on—aren't problems to your German

Be strong and consistent when enforcing your household rules. It's important that you are in charge, not your Shepherd.

Photo by Isabelle Francais.

Shepherd. Your dog digs because the dirt smells good, because the weather is hot, and he wants to lie in some cooler dirt, or because you have gophers that he would like to play with. All of the things that you consider problems, your Shepherd is doing for a reason. However, that doesn't mean that there is nothing you can do. Most problem behavior can be worked with; if it cannot be stopped entirely, it can be controlled or prevented.

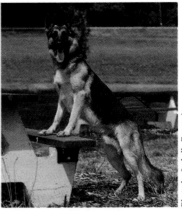

Training can often prevent disruptive behaviors such as barking and jumping from becoming a problem.

TRAINING

Training can play a big part in controlling problem behavior. A fair yet firm training program teaches your dog that you are in charge, that he is below you in the family, and should reinforce his concept of you as a kind, calm, caring leader. You can also use your training skills to teach your dog what is acceptable and what is not.

WHAT CAN YOU DO?

Health Problems

Some experts feel that 20 percent of all behavior problems commonly seen are caused by health-related problems. A bladder infection commonly causes housetraining problems. Medications can cause behavior changes. Sometimes thyroid problems can cause a behavior problem, so can hyperactivity, hormone imbalances, and a variety of other health problems. If you have some concerns about your dog's physical health, make an appointment with your veterinarian.

To help channel your puppy's energy into positive pursuits, make sure he gets enough attention and exercise.

Nutrition

Nutrition often plays a part in problem behavior. If your dog is not eating a good quality food, or if he isn't digesting his food properly, his body may be missing some vital nutrients. If your Shepherd is chewing on rocks or wood, is eating the stucco off the side of your house, grazing on the plants in your backyard, or is eating dirt, he may have a nutritional problem. Some dogs develop a type of hyperactivity when they eat a high calorie, high fat, high protein dog food. Other dogs have food allergies that might show up as behavior problems. If you have any questions about your dog's behavior in relation to food, or about the food you are feeding your dog, ask your veterinarian.

Play

Play is different from exercise, although exercise can be play. Laughter is very much a part of play and that is what makes it so special. Researchers know that laughter is wonderful medicine—it makes you feel better—and because of that, it has a special place in your relationship with your dog. If training is sometimes

Health problems can sometimes cause behavioral problems. One of the fundamentals of your German Shepherd's good health is a sound, healthy diet. Photo courtesy of Nutro Products, Inc.

difficult, and your dog is getting into trouble, make time to play with him. Play is a great stress reliever, both for you and for your dog, so make some time every day to laugh and play.

Sometimes dogs will intentionally get into trouble because they feel ignored. To some dogs, negative attention (corrections, yelling, and screaming) is better than no attention. By setting aside some time just for your Shepherd, you can avoid some of these situations.

EXERCISE

Exercise is just as important for your Shepherd as it is for you. It works the body, uses up excess energy, relieves stress, and clears the mind. How much exercise and what type depends upon your dog. A fast-paced walk might be enough exercise for a senior Shepherd but a young, healthy adult German Shepherd will need a good run or a fast-paced game of ball. Maybe even a fast-paced game of ball after a good run!

If your Shepherd has some physical limitations or if you have any doubts about his exercise needs, talk to your veterinarian. When you start an exercise program, start gradually, especially if your dog has been a couch potato. Sore muscles are no fun.

Play and exercise in whatever form you and your Shepherd enjoy will help keep him healthy and out of trouble.

Photo by Isabelle Francais.

A dog that is as large as the German Shepherd must be taught good manners and proper behavior—for his safety and the safety of others.

german shepherd

PREVENT PROBLEMS FROM HAPPENING

Because so many of the things we consider problems are not problems to your dog, you need to prevent them from happening as much as possible when you are not there to teach him. If your Shepherd finds out how much fun it is to chew up your sofa cushion, throwing stuffing all over, you may have a difficult time stopping him. The same applies to the kitchen trash can that is full of scraps (treasures to your food-motivated Shepherd!), the fruit trees in the back yard, and the children's toys. It's much easier to prevent a problem from happening than it is to break a bad habit.

Preventing a problem from happening might require you to fence off the garden, build some new, higher shelves in the garage, or maybe even build your Shepherd a new dog run.

Part of preventing problems from happening also requires that you limit your dog's freedom. A young puppy or an untrained dog should never have unsupervised free run of the house; there is just too much he can get into. Instead, keep him in the room with you either by watching him or better yet, using baby gates across the doorways. If you can't keep him with you, then put him in his crate or outside in his yard.

HOUSEHOLD RULES

You may even need to institute some new household rules for you and other family members. Your dog can't raid the trash cans if you take the trash cans out before they are overflowing and put the trash cans away before you leave the house. Your Shepherd would get into less trouble if everyone would close closet doors, pick up dirty laundry, and pick up their toys.

DEALING WITH SPECIFIC PROBLEMS

Digging and Destroying the Garden

If your back yard looks like a military artillery range, you need to concentrate first on preventing these things from happening when you are not there to supervise your dog. If you come home eight to ten hours later and try to correct your dog for the hole he dug when you left for work, you are wasting your time; your correction is much too late. Instead of understanding that he is being corrected for digging, your Shepherd is going to think he's being corrected for you coming home.

BUILD YOUR SHEPHERD A DOG RUN

Make the run big enough so that he can move around and trot back and forth. Make sure there is shade, unspillable water, and shelter from bad weather. When you leave him in the run, give him a toy or a treat and leave a radio on a soft, easy listening station in a nearby window.

When you're home, let your dog out for supervised runs in the backyard. When he starts to get into trouble, you can interrupt his actions and teach him what is acceptable and what is not.

The destructive dog also needs exercise, training, and play time every day to use up energy, stimulate his mind, and spend time with you. Most importantly, don't let your canine landscape artist watch you garden; if you do, he will come to you later with all of those bulbs you planted earlier!

The Barker

Are your neighbors complaining because your dog is serenading the neighborhood

Dog toys are a great way to keep your energetic Shepherd busy and happy.

german shepherd

Photo by Isabelle Francais.

Provide your Shepherd with a place of his own for exercise and unsupervised time by building him a dog run.

outside, out front, and have your neighbor come out and talk. Maybe the kids can play and create a distraction. When your dog barks, run back home as fast as you can and correct him again. Repeat as often as you need until he understands.

Some dogs will stop barking as you leave if you make leaving home very low-key and unexciting. A distraction also works well for many dogs. Take a small brown paper lunch bag and put a couple of treats in it, maybe a dog biscuit, a piece of carrot, a slice of apple, and a small toy. Tape the top shut and rip a very tiny hole in the side of the bag. As you walk out the door or the gate, give this to your Shepherd. He will be so busy trying to figure out what's

when you're at work? Shepherds typically are not problem barkers, but they will bark if bored and lonely.

Start by teaching him to be quiet while you're at home. When your dog starts barking, tell him "Quiet!" When he stops barking, praise him, "Good boy to be quiet!"

When he understands what you want, go for a short walk outside, leaving your dog at home. Listen, and when you hear him start barking, come back and correct him. After a few corrections, when your dog seems to have the idea, ask your neighbor to help you. Go

Many dogs will bark if they are bored or lonely. If your Shepherd is barking and annoying the neighbors, work on his behavior with correction and praise.

inside that he won't pay attention to you leaving.

EXTRA HELP

Problem barkers may need extra help. There are anti-bark collars on the market and several are humane and effective. All are triggered by the dog's barking and administer a correction to the dog. Some collars make a high pitched sound, one squirts a whiff of citronella and others administer an electric shock. I do not recommend the shock treatment for most dogs; many will panic when corrected this way. However, the first two collars are quite effective with many dogs.

Dashing Through Doors and Gates

This is actually one of the easiest problems to correct. Teach your Shepherd to sit and stay at all doors and gates, then to hold that stay until you either give him permission to go through or after you have closed the door. By teaching him that doors and gates are boundaries that require permission, you will eliminate the problem.

Start with your dog on a leash and walk him up to the door. Have him sit, tell him to stay, and then with the leash firmly grasped in your hand, open the door wide and stand aside. If he dashes forward, correct him for breaking his stay, "No, stay!" Take him back where he started and do it again. If he continues to do it, give him a snap and release of the leash and collar as you correct him verbally. When he will hold the stay at this door, go to other doors and gates and teach the same lesson, the same way.

If your Shepherd tries to sneak past you when he is not on the leash, block him with your leg or slam the door in his face as you give him a verbal correction.

If your dog does make it outside, don't chase him. If you chase him it becomes a game. Use your shaker to call him to you, "Sweetie, do you want a cookie? Come! Good boy!" When you do catch him or he comes back to you, don't correct him. If you do, he learns that coming back to you results in a correction. Instead, praise him for coming to you.

Jumping on People

Shepherds are solid, muscular dogs that can cause great damage if they jump on people. Your Shepherd can't jump on you or other people if

*To prevent your eager Shepherd from dashing through doors ahead of you,
teach him to sit and stay at the door until he is released.*

german shepherd

he's sitting; it's physically impossible to do both things at the same time. Since your dog jumps on people for attention, if you teach him to sit when you pet him you can eliminate the jumping.

When you come home from work and your dog is excited to see you, don't try to greet him with your arms full. Instead, greet him with empty hands. Then, when he tries to jump, grab him by the collar or the scruff of the neck and tell him to sit. When he sits, praise him, "Good boy to sit!" and pet him. If he tries to jump up again, use your hands to put him back into the sitting position.

If your Shepherd is really excited and it's very hard for him to control himself, roll him over onto his back once he's sitting and give him a belly rub and a massage. This is still giving him the attention he needs but it is relaxing him at the same time.

You can also use the leash to teach your Shepherd not to jump. When you are out for a walk and see your neighbor, don't let your neighbor pet your Shepherd until you make him sit. If he starts to jump on your neighbor, use a snap and release of the leash and a verbal correction, "No jump! Sit." Use the same technique when guests come to your house (leash your dog before they come in).

The key to correcting jumping is to make sure that the bad behavior is not rewarded. If someone pets your Shepherd when he jumps up, the bad behavior is rewarded. When he learns that he gets all of the attention when he's sitting, then he will start sitting automatically for petting, and when he does, praise him enthusiastically!

OTHER PROBLEMS?

Many behavior problems can be solved, or at least controlled, by using similar techniques. Try to figure out why your Shepherd is doing what he's doing (from his point of view, not yours), what you can do to prevent the problem from happening, and what you can do to use your training skills to teach your dog. Remember that a correction alone will not solve the problem; you need to prevent the problem as much as possible and also teach your dog what he can do.

If you still have some unsolved problems or if your dog is showing aggressive tendencies, contact your local dog trainer or behaviorist for expert help.

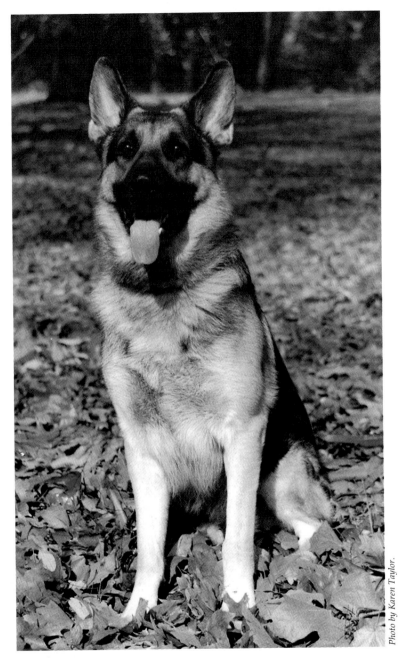

Photo by Karen Taylor.

A well-behaved German Shepherd is a pleasure to own. Remember that affection and praise are your dog's best motivation.

german shepherd

Have Some
FUN
With Your Training!

RETRIEVING

Most German Shepherds are good retrievers, willing and able to bring back anything that moves or is thrown. However, some will chase after whatever is thrown but don't always bring it back. If your Shepherd likes to retrieve, then all you need to do is fine-tune the game so that he brings the item all the way back to you and gives it to you without playing tug-of-war. If he hesitates on the way back, simply call him to you. If he drops the item, send him back to it, again using encouragement to have him pick it up and bring it to you. Don't scold him or try to correct him; that will only serve to discourage him.

If your dog likes to take the thrown item and run with it, playing keep away, you have

German Shepherds make great retrievers and are always ready for a game of Frisbee™ or catch.

Photo by Karen Taylor.

Once your dog has mastered basic obedience, he can accomplish just about anything. This Shepherd has some fun maneuvering through a tire of a trainer's obstacle course.

two options. You can stop the game and go inside, leaving him alone. This shows him that you will not chase him and the game will end when he tries to play keep away. Or you can have a long leash (a length of clothesline rope) on him when you start the game so that if he tries to play keep away, you can step on the rope, stop him, and use the rope to bring him back to you. If you need to use the rope, you still must praise him for coming back to you even if you made him do it. As has been said previously, the come must be positive.

USE TOYS MADE FOR DOGS

Nylabone® Frisbees™ made especially for dogs are great fun. Throw the Frisbee™ and encourage your dog to chase it. When he jumps up after it, praise him enthusiastically. Go to a toy store and look in the aisle where Frisbees™ and balls are displayed. There are a variety of toys there that can make good retrieving dog toys; just keep your dog's safety in mind.

Once your Shepherd is retrieving reliably and bringing the toy back to you, there are

If your dog would rather run with the ball than bring it back to you, try keeping him on long leash to prevent him from getting away.

Photo by Isabelle Francais.

german shepherd

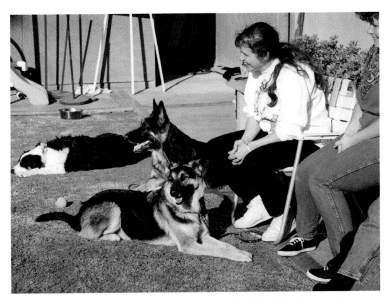

Training should be fun for both you and your Shepherd, but keep sessions short and take periodic breaks from the action.

unlimited games you can play. Most German Shepherds are enthusiastic about tennis balls, so that is the obvious game of choice for many. To make it challenging, tennis balls can be thrown short or far, or bounced off the side of the house. If your Shepherd is really dedicated, throw several tennis balls and see how many he can pick up and carry at once!

THE NAME GAME

The name game is a great way to make your dog think. And don't doubt him for a minute, your dog can think and is capable of learning the names of many different items and people. Not only is this a great game for your Shepherd, but it can come in handy around the house. Tell your dog to find your keys, or your shoes. Send your Shepherd after the remote control to the television, or to go find mom or dad. Plus, it's great fun to show off to your friends or guests!

Start with two items that are very different, perhaps a tennis ball and a bowl. Sit on the floor with your Shepherd and those two items, and have some treats that he likes. Tell him, "Where's the ball?" and bounce the ball so that he tries to grab it or at least pays attention to it. When he touches it, tell him,

Enjoy! A productive training process will only strengthen the bond between you and your German Shepherd.

critical step in his learning process and you may need to repeat it several times.

When he will pick up his ball from among several different items, including other toys, then start hiding the ball. Make it simple to start, maybe just partially hidden under a magazine. As he gets better, start making it more challenging.

THE COME GAME

In this game, two family members will stand or sit across the room or yard from each other. Each will have some treats for your Shepherd. Taking turns, each will call your dog to come and when he does, praise and reward him. This is a very simple game but gives you a chance to practice the come command and makes it fun at the same time. Plus, everyone in the family can practice it, giving even the kids a chance to "train" your dog.

"Good boy to find the ball!" and give him a treat.

When he is responding to the ball, lay it on the floor next to the bowl and send him after it. Praise and reward him for getting it. Now set several different items out with the bowl and ball and send him again. When he brings back the ball, praise and reward him. When he is doing that well, place one of his toys out there, too, and send him. If he goes for his other toy, take it away, with no comment, and send him after the ball again. This is a

The come command can be practiced and even turned into a game when you and other family members take turns calling to your dog.

When you can hide the tennis ball and your dog can find it, start teaching him the names of other items, following the same process. You will find that the first three items will be the most difficult. Your dog needs to master the learning process and he needs to understand the concept you are trying to teach him. Once he understands that each of these things has a different sound, and that he needs to listen to you say those sounds, then he will start learning much faster.

Young or old, your German Shepherd will take pride in learning and performing new commands and tricks.

Photo by Isabelle Francais.

Wherever they are, German Shepherds are ready for games like hide and seek. Teaching them some basic obedience skills will give you more choices for fun.

HIDE AND SEEK

Hide and seek is a fun game, much like the hide and seek you played as a child, except that you (or other family members) will hide and your Shepherd will find you. Your dog will be much better at finding than you ever were, though, because he has such a sensitive nose and outstanding scenting abilities.

Start by teaching a family member's name (or your own) using the techniques you learned in the name game. When your dog can identify a family member, you can use that family member to hide. Give that family member a treat and have him show your dog that he has one. Hold your

Shepherd as that family member goes and hides in a fairly easy location. Tell your dog, "Go find dad!" and let him go. If he starts to look around and sniff, just be quiet and let him work and think. If your dog starts to look flustered or confused, tell him again, "Go find dad!" and help him find him. When he goes to dad, praise him enthusiastically and let dad give your dog the treat.

As your dog gets better at this game, you can start making it more challenging. Have family members hide in more difficult places or slightly farther away from your Shepherd. They can also run around a little before finding a hiding place, so that there is a more challenging trail. As your Shepherd gets better, you can also cover his eyes so that he can't see the family member go hide.

When your dog has learned the names of different family members and knows how to find them, you can use this skill around the house. Send your Shepherd out to the yard to get the kids when it's dinner time. Or have him take the TV remote control to dad when he asks for it. Hide and seek is a lot of fun, challenging for your dog, and uses his natural scenting abilities.

SHAKE HANDS

Shaking hands is a very easy trick to teach your dog. Have your Shepherd sit in front of you and ask him to "Shake" as you reach behind one front paw and tickle his leg in the hollow just behind his paw. When he lifts his paw to escape the tickle, shake his paw as you tell him, "Good to shake!" and give him a treat. When he starts to lift his paw on his own, stop tickling.

WAVE

When he is shaking hands reliably, tell him "Shake. Wave!" and instead of shaking his paw, just lightly touch your hand under his paw and move your hand away so that he continues to reach for your hand. As he reaches for your hand, tell him, "Good to wave!" With the wave, you want him to lift his paw higher than in the shake and to move it up and down so that he looks like he is waving.

TREAT ON NOSE

Have your Shepherd sit and stay. Hold his chin with one hand as you place a treat on the top of his nose. Tell him "Stay!" After a few seconds, tell him, "Okay!" and let him toss the treat and catch it. Gradually increase the time you want him to wait before you release him and enthusiastically praise him when he catches the treat in mid-air.

ROLL OVER

Have your Shepherd lie down. With a treat in one hand, circle your Shepherd's head with the treat in the direction you want him to roll, while you tell him, "Roll over!" At first, you may need to physically help him roll. Praise him when he does roll over, even if you need to help him. Enthusiastically praise him when he does it on his own.

Once he can roll over by himself, you can ask him to do it more than once. Have him roll over two or three times. Teach him a command for each, "Three roll overs!" or "Two roll overs!" Impress your friends that your dog knows how to count!

AND THERE'S MORE!

Trick training is limited only to what you want to teach your dog. Teach him to crawl, to play dead, or to sit up and beg. Teach him to dance. What would you (and your dog!) enjoy?

Whether he's retrieving, shaking hands, or rolling over, your German Shepherd will be thrilled to have your time and attention.

Photo by Isabelle Francais.

SUGGESTED READING

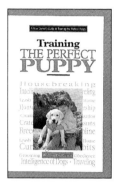

JG-109
Training The Perfect Puppy
By Andrew DePrisco
160 pages, over 200 color photos

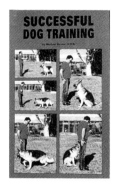

TS-205
Successful Dog Training
By Michael Kamer, OSB
160 pages, over 150 color photos

TS-258
Training Your Dog for Sports and
  Other Activities
By Charlotte Schwartz
160 pages, 170 full-color photos

TW-113
Everybody Can Train
  Their Own Dog
By Angela White
256 pages, 200 color photos

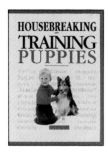

WW-009
Housebreaking and Training Puppies
By J.R. Gardner
64 pages, 79 full-color photos

WW-025
Dog Obedience Training
By Ross Allan
64 pages, over 100 full-color photos

TS-252
Dog Behavior and Training
By Lowell Ackerman, DVM
288 pages, over 170 full-color photos

KW-022
Basic Dog Training
By Miller Watson
96 pages, over 100 full-color photos

JG-117
Dog Training
By Dorman Pantfoeder
160 pages, over 100 full-color photos

TS-283
Training Problem Dogs
By Dr. Louis Vine
256 pages, 50 drawings

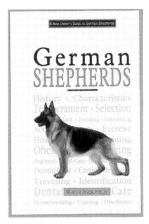

JG-102
A New Owner's Guide to German Shepherds
Charlotte Schwartz
160 pages, 150 full-color photos

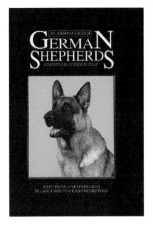

BB-102
Dr. Ackerman's Book of German Shepherds
Lowell Ackerman, DVM
96 pages, 75 full-color photos

PS-810
Book of the German Shepherd
Ernest H. Hart
256 pages

TW-144
The Proper Care of German Shepherds
Dr. Carmen Battaglia
256 pages, more than 240 full-color photos